INDEFINITE POSTPONEMENT

INDEFINITE POSTPONEMENT

A Case Study of Adolescent Suicidality

JOHN P. WILLIAMS, MD

PRESSED WAFER
Brooklyn

PRESSED WAFER
375 Parkside Avenue, Brooklyn, NY 11226
www.pressedwafer.com

ISBN: 978-1-940396-37-8

First Edition · January 2018
Printed in the United States of America

For Ellen

CONTENTS

ACKNOWLEDGMENTS

MANY PEOPLE have made this book possible. I thank Matthew Schuerman, Lila Williams, Jane Williams, Dr. John Heon, Dr. David P. Williams III, James Melia, Bill Corbett, and Beverly Corbett for their edits of and comments on the manuscript, and I am especially grateful to Dr. Judith Beck for her foreword. Each added much to the work. They also encouraged me to complete it, a labor that was often carried out at odd hours under less than favorable circumstances.

I also thank James Byrne, Esq., who—indirectly—inspired me to create the 501(c)(3) entity that will handle the disbursement of profits that accrue from the book's publication, all of which will be donated to other charities dedicated to the prevention of suicide.

I most of all thank Grace, who gave the written consent that has allowed me to publish her diary in this format. Although I have guaranteed her that I will always maintain her confidentiality, it took incredible courage for her to release such a personal document. As I told her many times, we will save lives with this book, and we already have.

FOREWORD

WE HAVE A SUICIDE CRISIS in the United States. It has come upon us without much fanfare, and its causes remain unclear. In the past fifteen years, deaths from suicide have risen sharply even as mortality from cancer has fallen. We have new medications for cancer, but no comparable treatment to prevent suicide.

Why?

I suspect that there are several reasons. First, there is just not enough research on suicide. The number of clinical trials monitored by the National Institutes of Health involving the term "cancer" dwarfs those with the word "suicide" by a factor of sixty-eight to one.[1] In contrast, deaths from cancer in the United States in 2014 only surpassed mortality from suicide by a factor of fourteen to one.[2]

Second, many suicidal individuals and their families are afraid to talk about suicidality, fearing discrimination in the workplace and disapproval or even isolation from society at large. Third, because of factors including a dearth of mental health clinicians, a lack of proper training, and poor mental health insurance coverage, far too few who need care receive it. Fourth, an unprecedented array of societal stressors including economic stagnation and a rise in substance abuse have led many to contemplate suicide.

To prevent suicide we have to understand its psychopathology, and presently, there is only one way to accomplish this: by documenting the thoughts of those who wish to die. In 1979, Dr. Aaron Beck created the Scale of Suicidal Ideation, in which the clinician captures the thoughts of a client on a range of topics including wish to live, desire to attempt, duration of ideation, and deterrents. As with all clinician-administered scales, the practitioner only knows the thoughts that a client chooses to share, which can create an inherent barrier to understanding suicidality.

Consider, however, if a suicidal client's thoughts were captured *not* in the recollective space of a psychotherapy appointment but as they happened. Then suppose that a clinician were to organize and interpret those thoughts. Significant insight into suicidality might be the result. This is exactly what a young woman named Grace and her psychiatrist, Dr. Williams, have provided with *Indefinite Postponement*.

For reasons that remain obscure, Grace decided to record her descent in the form of a memoir. It appears that she had no interest in sharing it with anyone, especially not her initial therapist. Then, she revealed its existence to Dr. Williams, who has written a commentary around it.

The resulting document is a compelling and important perspective on not only adolescent suicidality but the disorder in general. There have been numerous academic books written on the topic and many fewer published diaries from suicidal clients. What is rare and likely unique about the present book is that it combines the perspectives of the treating clinician *and* the client.

When treating a suicidal patient, clinicians should first use evidence-based practices.[3] These approaches, however, may not work, or work well enough, with some suicidal clients. In all cases a thorough understanding of the phenomenology of suicide is important.

Indefinite Postponement contains many insights for the clinician, emphasizing the necessity of listening and suggesting what to do and what not to do in caring for suicidal clients. The audience for this work, however, extends far beyond licensed professionals and trainees. Suicidal clients and their families can learn much from it.

Over the course of *Indefinite Postponement*, Grace decides against suicide. There is no simple reason for this, and as the title indicates, a reversal remains possible. Nevertheless, Grace postponed her suicide indefinitely and remains alive today.

This book holds out hope that suicidality can be temporary and that it can be overcome. If the reason behind it can be discerned and addressed, the urge to die can fade. To the many who suffer in silence, thinking that they are totally alone and ready to give up, this book's message is that you are not alone and that you do not have to give up.

You can find someone to listen, to understand, and to help. There is hope.

JUDITH BECK, PhD
President, Beck Institute for Cognitive Behavior Therapy
Clinical Professor of Psychology in Psychiatry, University of Pennsylvania
February 2017

INDEFINITE POSTPONEMENT

INTRODUCTION

WHEN I FINISHED my postgraduate medical education, I found that I knew little about suicide. I had learned about depression, anxiety, psychosis, and substance abuse, but the sometime endpoint of these conditions was not widely discussed, especially in the first and second years of training. I could have read about the topic in my spare time, but it was not something that I gravitated toward. Perhaps I felt that avoidance would offer protection from the outcome that all of us residents feared would take hold of our patients—or perhaps, having never had suicidal impulses myself, I had difficulty imagining that someone, least of all one of *my* patients, could end her life.

During my training after medical school, a fellow physician attempted suicide and survived, but even then, there was no open examination of the issue. I can understand the omission, as there were issues of confidentiality regarding an individual whom everyone knew and whose career might be negatively affected were the news to spread.

We should have talked about it, considering that physicians are more likely than the general population to die by suicide and may especially be put at risk by the emotional stress of the job.[1] Had we done so, we might have taken an important step toward meeting one of the greatest challenges we face with our patients: talking about suicide, not being scared by it, and being better able to battle it.

Why wasn't the topic discussed, in that moment of crisis or more generally? The problem is systemic. The days, hours, and minutes of medical residents are tightly scripted by a bureaucracy known as the Accreditation Council for Graduate Medical Education (ACGME), which dictates the topics that must be covered in postgraduate medical training. At first, these were guidelines, but the ACGME now spells out not only what should be taught but also how residents—not just in psychiatry, but in every medical specialty, from anesthesiology to urology—should be instructed so that they demonstrate "competencies."

In writing this book, I read through the latest distillation of the ACGME's guidance for psychiatry training, known as *The Psychiatry Milestone Project*.[2] The words "competence," "competency," "competencies," "subcompetency," and "subcompetencies" appear seventeen times in the document; words related to suicide appear twice. Residents who have mastered "Level 1" of the "PC1" competency domain, Psychiatric Evaluation, should be able to screen for patient safety, including suicidal ideation. Residents who have mastered "Level 2" will know how to assess for patient safety, including suicidal ideation. The concept of suicidality is never mentioned again in the *Milestone Project* document.

It is disturbing that two mentions in the ACGME's manifesto encapsulate the entirety of the group's standard for a psychiatry resident's competency around suicide. Cardiology patients die from heart attacks, and oncology patients die from cancer. Our patients die from suicide, and although it may be sufficient for an internal medicine and family practice doctor to do no more than screen and assess for suicidality, I believe that psychiatrists will fall far short in reducing suicide if screening and assessing for suicide are the only competencies that must be demonstrated.

"Are you suicidal?" asks the psychiatry resident.

"No," says the patient.

"OK. Good. Let's move on."

It sounds like a joke, but it is not. Suicide is a topic that few people outside of the psychiatric field want to discuss. When I've mentioned at dinner parties that I've been writing this book, the effect is mostly one of indigestion and then secondarily, one of sick humor. My more polite guests/hosts will appear interested, but few people want to hear about the topic. It's just, you know… depressing. Psychiatrists are people too, and therefore it's only natural that they veer away from the topic.

The words "ethics" and "ethical" appear thirteen times in the *Milestone Project* document, which raises a question: Do not ethics require that the template for psychiatry residency makes central the most important role of the psychiatrist—keeping one's patients from death at their own hands? I mean no offense to the ACGME, but we face a catastrophe in the epidemiology of suicide, and the Council's members may just read this.

In 1986 there were 12.5 deaths per 100,000 people in the United States from suicide, and that number fell to 10.5 deaths per 100,000 by 1999—a 16 percent reduction.[3]

Then something odd happened—the number started rising, continuously. In 2014, the last year for which we currently have data from the Centers for Disease Control and Prevention (CDC), the rate was 13.0 deaths per 100,000, 2.5 higher than 1999's rate, representing a 23.8 percent increase. In comparison, deaths from cancer from 1999 to 2013 fell from 200.8 to 163.2 per 100,000—a reduction of 18.7 percent.[4]

3

In every age cohort defined by the CDC from ten to seventy-four, the rate of completed suicide rose from 1999 to 2014. The rates of increase are alarming, especially for females.

MALES

10- to 14-year-old cohort: 36.8 percent;
15- to 24-year-old cohort: 8.3 percent;
25- to 44-year-old cohort: 12.5 percent;
55- to 64-year-old cohort: 42.8 percent;
65- to 74-year-old cohort: 7.7 percent.

FEMALES

10- to 14-year-old cohort: 200.0 percent;
15- to 24-year-old cohort: 53.3 percent;
25- to 44-year-old cohort: 30.9 percent;
55- to 64-year-old cohort: 63.3 percent;
65- to 74-year-old cohort: 43.9 percent.

In 2013, the rate of suicidal death varied widely by state/territory, from 5.7 per 100,000 in Washington, DC, to 23.7 in Montana. Firearms remain a major driver of completed suicide; states with strict firearms laws vs. permissive laws enjoy an annual reduction of approximately 6.25 suicide deaths per 100,000.[5] This is notable when one recalls that the overall 2014 rate of suicide death was 13.0 per 100,000 nationally. Firearms, however, have long been readily available to the American suicide contemplator and therefore do not explain the rise in suicide deaths since 1999. Although the federal assault weapons ban expired in 2004, and such weapons can now be purchased in many states with relative ease, it is unlikely that most suicidalists—at least, those who intend only to take their own lives—would employ an AR-15.[6]

Education and income—and the lack of both—may also play a role in the increase. From 1999 to 2013, among non-Hispanic whites aged forty-five to fifty-four with at least a bachelor of arts degree, the mortality rate from suicide rose 3.3 percent; for those of the same age with a high school diploma or less, the increase was 17.0 percent.[7] The correlation between education and income is well known, with the Bureau of Labor Statistics estimating average weekly earnings in 2014 of $488 for those without a high school diploma and $1,639 for those with a professional degree.[8] Furthermore, long-term unemployment, especially within the first five years of a job loss, is correlated with an increased risk of suicide.[9] If the cause of increased suicidality were purely economic, however, one would not expect to see such a large increase in suicide completion among ten- to fourteen-year-olds. Additionally, one would not expect suicide necessarily to become the leading killer of adolescent girls worldwide.[10]

In 2009, I encountered my first case of an adolescent patient made suicidal by use of social networking sites (SNS). She wasn't "cyberbullied," but she was depressed because others had more "likes" on their pages than she did. When she told me about this, I was surprised, but the largest study of this subject to date confirms the connection between the use of SNS and suicidal ideation and attempts. Put another way, simply using SNS may make some people suicidal.[11] This has certainly been my experience in clinical practice.

There are many other well-known risk factors for suicide, including family history, substance abuse, traumatic brain injury, and sexual or physical abuse. Nevertheless, some patients present with no discernible risk factors and still want to kill themselves. Why? As my grandfather used to say, "If something doesn't make sense, you don't have all the facts."

I have found that patients often fail to give the reason for their suicidality, usually because it is unknown to them. The drive to live is strong—or, at least, it is expected to be so. Its absence appears to be a uniquely human phenomenon. Despite the stories of sheep jumping from cliffs and cats from bridges, actual suicide has never been demonstrated in a species other than man.[12] The stigma associated with mental illness and suicidality has been well documented, and this shame may prevent patients from communicating why they wish to end their lives.[13] Suicide needs to be discussed—without shame or stigma, and with the certainty that one's liberty will not be lost.

As a psychiatrist, I long feared the patient who would walk into my office with the strong desire to kill herself—with no apparent reason why. What follows is the story of exactly such a patient, whom I will call Grace. If I had been a better doctor, I would have solved her riddle a lot more quickly than I did. Only luck prevented her death. I write this book—with the full, written consent of my patient and with our commitment that all profits be donated to charities dedicated to suicide prevention—so that other professionals, parents, siblings, and friends might not have to be quite so lucky.

Grace's identity will never be known, and she has not sat in my office for many years, but I frequently think about her and how close she came to death. Looking back at her crisis from the vantage of recovery, she told me:

I already was a living corpse.

I knew little when I treated her, but now, because of her, perhaps a bit more.

PART ONE

GRACE was born in Ireland (not her real country), and had lived in Maryland (not her real state of residence) for most of her fifteen years when she came to my office some years ago. She was referred by a colleague for acute suicidality. I knew something about the topic; I had already spent four years as an emergency room psychiatrist at the VA Medical Center in Philadelphia and had treated one highly suicidal adolescent while a fellow in child psychiatry. Grace looked normal enough. She wasn't catatonic, and she smiled frequently. She even made jokes.

Then she got down to business. She wanted to die and had for the past nine months. She had no present plan to take her life, but this was not for lack of desire or capability. She had deferred attempting because she suspected that she would not succeed. This was the sole thread suspending her above the abyss, and she made it clear in that first session that when success could be guaranteed, she would do what she needed to do. She was a burden to her family and friends, and they would be better off when she was dead. "I'm so sick of myself," she said. When she could find a plan that would work, she would execute it, and that could be next year or next week.

Grace admitted that she had been psychotic, with frequent hallucinations and a sense of grandiosity, which at times included the sense that she could succeed in killing herself.

Although only in tenth grade, she was already taking calculus, and her mind displayed a ruthless, almost computational efficiency. When she finally made her attempt, it would be planned, well executed, and successful.

Although little was said of it in the first meeting, Grace was seeing another psychiatrist, whom I will call Dr. Geeringer, for psychotherapy and medication management, and my task was to provide a second opinion. Diagnosed with major depressive disorder, Grace was medicated with lithium, a mood stabilizer; Seroquel, an antipsychotic; Effexor, an antidepressant; and clonazepam, a sedative. This was a curious combination. Although lithium, Seroquel, and Effexor may have a role in the treatment of depression, benzodiazepines, including clonazepam, may worsen the condition.[1] According to Grace, none of the drugs seemed to be doing much good. As one after another medication was added, she felt increasingly groggy but no less suicidal.

I knew my principal recommendation within the first five minutes of the assessment: Grace had to be hospitalized. Although patients face an increased risk of death from suicide following psychiatric hospitalization, and its survival benefit is questionable, a psychiatrist who encounters a psychotic patient with acute suicidality and doesn't hospitalize will—in the case of an adverse outcome—be squarely in the realm of malpractice. Such care might even be grossly negligent, which is to say highly deviant from the expected treatment.

Before I had the chance to make my suggestion and emergently terminate the evaluation, Grace stated that she would not be voluntarily hospitalized. She said it abruptly, as if she anticipated my coming assault and was responding first with a flanking maneuver. If I forced the issue and involuntarily committed her, she suggested that she could immediately kill herself after discharge. For Grace, the loss of control was connected to her suicidality; as she felt more of the former, there was more of the latter.

When I was a psychiatry resident, I was taught to commit a patient who was highly suicidal but refused admission. (When suicide was covered as a topic in the didactic portion of my training, it seemed mostly from a medicolegal perspective.) Involuntary hospitalization was the so-called standard of care, a legal term denoting the necessary medical ministrations that a psychiatrist had to provide to avoid negligence. This left me with two options.

A: Commit Grace and be legally protected, knowing that I would never see her again, either because she would choose another psychiatrist who listened to his patients or because she would kill herself after discharge.

B: Not commit her and roll the dice, knowing that she might kill herself even if I didn't commit her and that I would then be defenseless in court—and she would be dead.

As the three-hour evaluation dragged on, I listened with increasing dread. When I took my customary break at ninety minutes, I went to the men's room and felt like I was going to vomit. Then I remembered the third law of *The House of God*: "At a cardiac arrest, the first procedure is to take your own pulse."[2] I splashed water on my face and returned to my office.

I sat down and continued listening to Grace. She began talking freely about all the antagonists in her life: school, enemies, friends, frenemies, her family, and the complete hopelessness of everything. She was irredeemably negative, but the fluidity of her conversation gave me hope in that she appeared to feel safe enough to share her thoughts of death. That was positive. Maybe she would also feel comfortable calling me when she was ready to end everything, and I could stop her in the moment itself. Maybe Grace could actually be cured.

She also appeared increasingly animated as the interview proceeded. She was gaining energy, and, neophyte that I was, this reduced my concern. I wondered if my careful questioning and nonreactive listening were giving her hope. Although we had only spoken for two hours, perhaps my healing presence had given her a reason to live. The therapeutic relationship would save the day, and there would be a happy ending, with disaster efficiently averted.

Calmness flowed over me, but her rising vivacity should have alarmed me instead. Although I didn't know it at the time, patients may seem less sad and more energetic in the moments before a suicide attempt. This makes intuitive sense; killing one's self requires tremendous effort, something typically beyond the capabilities of the de-energized, depressed patient.

The data gathering ended, and I generated a list of treatment recommendations for Grace and her mother, whom I invited into the room at the conclusion of the evaluation. A psychiatrist is also supposed to supply a diagnosis at this point, but I was puzzled. She was clearly sad, but I couldn't tell if her symptomology was secondary to major depressive disorder or bipolar disorder, i.e., depression and mania together. And what about the hallucinations? Was she showing signs of early onset schizophrenia? Like most beginners I assumed that, because she was suicidal, she might have the beginnings of a borderline personality disorder. Maybe she was using drugs, even though she denied it, and I should insist on a urine toxicology screen. As it turned out, every one of my hypotheses was wrong, and the decision to hedge on the diagnosis was a good one. Given the real possibility that I might not see Grace again—either for lack of follow-up or worse—I faced the delicate task of balancing the confidentiality of a minor with the need to develop a family-based safety plan, however useless that might be. So I presented my ideas, and the patient and her mother listened. There were a lot of medication recommendations, as if I knew of a specific drug that could stop someone from jumping in front of a bus. I suggested cognitive behavioral therapy and its cousin, dialectical behavioral therapy—two psychotherapies that probably can reduce suicidality. I knew from Grace that Dr. Geeringer was a psychoanalyst, which meant that he was trained to practice a kind of talking therapy developed by Sigmund Freud and his followers. I have found Freud and psychodynamic therapy (a kind of simplified version of psychoanalysis) to be invaluable in treating certain conditions, not including suicidality.

My worst recommendation had to be my request that she call right away if the suicidality worsened. Who was I kidding? It already *had* worsened. I knew that there was a real chance that Grace might kill herself within the next week, and here I was, ignoring the very phenomenology that I had been trained—or not trained—to treat.

Grace's mother was well aware of her daughter's death wishes, which I sheepishly mentioned with the idea of commitment, but she had no desire to have her daughter hospitalized either. She added that Grace's father felt the same way. This lack of interest afforded me no protection; patients and their parents are not expected to know psychiatry.

Then they left. *Yes, we will call you right away if Grace doesn't feel safe.* Less than a minute later, I went to the waiting room to greet the next patient, whose identity is long forgotten. Though patients came and went for follow-up appointments the rest of the afternoon, I was still with Grace.

After I had written my report, I sent it to Dr. Geeringer, whom I imagined might be upset by it. He wasn't—or, at least, didn't appear to be. One of the greatest discoveries of psychoanalysis was understanding the importance of countertransference— how the therapist feels about the patient—and how to regulate and conceal it. We discussed the case in depth, and when we were done, my colleague thanked me for my recommendations. Whatever Dr. Geeringer might have thought of me, he controlled his countertransference, and our conversation was full of pleasantries. I was amiable enough. I knew that Grace lived and was safely (at least from the perspective of my own legal jeopardy) back in the care of her out-of-state psychiatrist.

In the subsequent weeks, I heard nothing more from Grace. I should have followed up in a timely fashion, even for a second opinion, but I didn't. Here was danger, and I avoided it. The leaves fell, and I encountered other suicidal patients, but none as concerning as Grace. By winter, I thought of her rarely, if at all.

The following summer, her mother contacted me, saying that Grace wanted to return to my care, which meant that she was alive. My first reaction was happiness and pride; maybe my initial assessment wasn't the therapeutic disaster I had assumed it to be. As with the rest of humanity, however, pride should be avoided by all physicians.

The elation quickly slid into fear. I had dodged a bullet, and the loaded gun of what I had assumed was a dismal prognosis was again aimed at my head. Then I considered the rather larger weapon aimed at Grace's, and scheduled her next appointment. My initial fear of her was fading, to be replaced by fascination.

Grace had seemed so likely to die but had not. Why? There I was, a bystander looking at another human leaning against a bridge girder and staring at the glistening bay, wondering how the impossibility of ending one's life became the possible and unremarkable, wondering when to jump. We control our destinies at every moment but, blessed by an illusion, remain mostly unaware of what we are capable of. With Grace, the myth was stripped away. In choosing not to die, she determined her fate continuously—and in doing so perhaps gained something. I wondered if she could only be truly alive knowing, in a visceral way, the continual possibility of her own death.

I saw her six times throughout the remainder of the year, making pharmacological suggestions and then advocating for electroconvulsive therapy (ECT). Although there is little pharmacological help for the treatment of suicidality per se, there are ample data on the efficacy of ECT in treating depression.[3] Dr. Geeringer was still the psychotherapist of record, but Grace didn't want to talk about medical therapies, pharmacological or otherwise.

She wanted to tell her story, not the whole thing, but parts of it.

Soon there were large puzzle pieces, laid before me in near apposition, as a mother might do for her below-average child. Looking back at my session notes, I see that everything she said made perfect sense and could have predicted Grace's actual problem and its cure. Nevertheless, I was oblivious to the pattern, even as it took on a greater resolution in front of me.

I wrote in my notes: "She continues to focus on control. If you lose control, then others will make decisions for you." Then: "She says that people are useless, and that is why she wants to die. There was only one person who was useful, a childhood friend called...." I responded to her statements by trying to convince her that she wasn't useless, that she had value, and that she was projecting the valuelessness she saw in others onto herself. The interpretation now seems idiotic and potentially fatal. I wrote, capturing her words: "Others will make decisions for you.... People are useless.... That is why she wants to die." If someone was useless, you got rid of him and found someone else who wasn't. Even if everyone on the planet was useless, you still had yourself—your sane self, protected and intact. Grace had one of those, didn't she? Her father and mother both looked blindingly unremarkable, her social development was typical, and her academic progress had been effortless before the onset of her illness and the lack of concentration it caused.

When I saw her next, a month later, I wrote: "She doesn't so much care about uselessness—and whether people are useful. 'I will just have to be useful for myself.' She says now that she has enough control." I was filled with a sense of hope. This wasn't just energy; she was gaining insight that would allow a permanent cure.

When I saw Grace again later in September and in October, however, her depression and anxiety were much worse, and shortly afterward she slit her wrists and nearly bled to death in her bathtub. This was unknown to me at the time, but when I heard nothing more from Grace and her family for another year, I assumed the worst and was not far off.

Then she called me and said that she would be moving to the area and asked whether we could commence weekly psychotherapy and medication management. I said yes, and we started a week later. Not long after, she revealed that she had tried to kill herself four times, three after the initial interview. This didn't surprise me. What did is that she had kept a diary throughout her entire illness, even at the points when death seemed inevitable. Like Nixon with his tapes, Grace fastidiously documented sadness, dismay, hopelessness, frustration, numbness, and grief from nearly the onset of her depression. Almost every moment of significance had been captured.

Much later, I asked her why she wrote it all down, and she told me that she wanted her family to have something to remember her by after her death. She also explained that she wanted others to understand that her suicide, once it occurred, had not been an impulsive act in response to a nasty boyfriend, a bad grade on a test, or some other transitory stressor. Instead, she wanted others to realize that she had planned things carefully and that her ultimate death was a kind of inevitability that could not have been prevented. As a result, her family members and friends would be unable to blame themselves for failing to stop her. She also said that the thing that scared her most about being dead was that she would not have the opportunity to explain why she chose death. Even worse, Dr. Geeringer might explain the reasons for Grace's death and get everything wrong. Thus, she wrote the diary.

Initially, this made as much sense to me as someone facing death from a disfiguring and incurable illness making careful preparations to preserve her corpse for daily inspection by the entire family. However illogically she wrote and preserved the diary, its existence creates the strangest and most insightful document of suicidality that I have read. One can look to Tumblr and find numerous postings from people in deep distress. Some of them may be truly suicidal; others may be fabricating such posts to garner clicks and eyeballs. Grace's diary is real. Despite the growing relevance of narrative to medicine generally, actual suicide diaries have rarely been the subject of scientific study. Searching the terms "suicide" and "diary" yields less than ten relevant papers in the entirety of the psychiatric literature. Sylvia Plath wrote extensively about her depression, but the unabridged version of her journals is silent for the last six months of her life.[4] The diaries of Cesar Pavese, an Italian writer, and Arthur Inman, a failed American poet, have also been analyzed to understand how they might explain the suicides that terminated both lives.[5]

There does not appear, however, to have ever been a published analysis of a suicide diary from an adolescent.

As she prepared to reveal the diary during treatment, Grace wrote to me:

> I have come to the realization that my fear about sharing [this] doesn't stem from what others would think, but rather from what I would think of myself if they knew. I think that I would be embarrassed and inclined to look down on myself if I gave it up. (Not that I don't already look down upon myself....) Putting up a façade is then, consequently, the easier option. Keeping secrets is easy for me because I am afraid of being vulnerable, and of losing control. I know all about confidentiality, but I am not sure if that applies here. I don't want my parents involved, and that is one of the reasons why I feel that it is safer that I keep this to myself. I have trust issues. Just adding to the burden is how painful this memory is to think about. It absolutely torments me. I feel uncomfortable and anxious and powerless every time it reoccurs. It is like I dissolve. I don't want talking about it to magnify this.
>
> I am afraid that letting you in will make it into a bigger problem than it already is for me. I am afraid of talking about the detail, because I don't want the memory to become more vivid. I don't want to know more about it. I am also afraid of not feeling validated, of people not believing me. In addition,

I am afraid, because when this has been suggested in the past, I have lied. I have lied to Dr. Geeringer, I have lied to Kate, and I have lied to you. In the end, the factor that keeps holding me back is that once those words leave my mouth, I can't take them back. I won't be able to lie my way out of this one like I do in so many other cases. It is easier to just keep it inside of me, where it doesn't have to come out. And that is my security. I am afraid of being hurt. I am not safe.

She would, after all that, tell me her story and more. As she recovered—the very act of telling the story the seeming cure—she started to write a new narrative critiquing her old diary and describing all the reasons why she didn't have to die. Grace's writings provide a remarkable clinical document exploring the nature of suicide, and her subsequent commentary on her suicide diary offers something that has not yet appeared in print. We hope that what follows will address one of the most pressing public health issues of our time, for both mental health professionals and lay people.

PART TWO

THE HURRICANE began with drizzle and a little wind:

> Sometimes I think of dying. I mean, when I was little, I was
> deathly afraid of, well, death. Some nights I would totally freak
> out because of it. But, when my parents asked, I would tell them
> that I was afraid of dinosaurs in the backyard. I doubt they
> bought that. As I grew older, I guess I forgot about dying or at
> least pushed it to the back burner. When I look back, the only
> things that I can remember about these panic episodes is that it
> was dark outside, and seeing through a white painted window
> and sitting on my mom's lap on the floor. And it wasn't even
> like I was faced with death. I hadn't experienced the passing
> of anyone or anything close to me. The thought that it would
> happen loomed over me.

This seemed inexplicable—a patient who was at once afraid
of death thinking about causing her own, imminently. If she
feared death, how could she seek her own? Wasn't anxiety a
protective factor against killing one's self? The link between
anxiety and suicide was only demonstrated in the psychiatric
literature when I was a second-year resident—but anxiety is,
in fact, a causative agent of suicidality.[1] Although the reasons
are unclear, those with an anxiety disorder are more than three
times as likely to attempt suicide as those without.

For Grace, however, the fear of death alone was not enough to impel her toward self-termination. Something else happened:

In third grade we had to put my cat to sleep. I was so angry at my parents because, no matter how they explained it, I could not grasp killing a living thing for its own benefit.

I can't clearly remember that cat, only the fact that I wanted it to live to have its seventh birthday in August, when he really died in February, the year after we had moved. I remember hugging him and saying goodbye to him in the backyard, still finding it hard to believe that he would not be coming back home with my mom. Afterwards, my dad took my sister and me upstairs to play Gamecube, and I stopped crying. Later we packed away his collar and toys in the basement in a trash bag, which I think is still there. I remember my mom cooking rice with canned asparagus for him when he stopped eating. Then we took him to the vet, and I remember hearing two possible diagnoses. One easily treated with medicine, and the other, cancer, which my parents would later tell me. When my mom told me that he was given poison to stop his heart, I refused to forgive them, making excuses in my mind to make it seem less true. Now all we have left is that trash bag, perhaps my sister's picture of him (she still cries over that), a box of ashes the same color as his fur, and a new cat waiting at the office stairs in his place.

Killing cats or any other animals for the sake of relieving their pain never makes much sense to most children, but they get over it. Most of them get another cat or a trampoline or an iPhone.

Grace didn't get over it. Instead, she was filled with anger because her parents, despite having no other apparent choice, violated what she saw at that point as the order of things. You don't kill to relieve pain, even if you think the subject would rather be dead. Animal euthanasia has long been a staple of veterinary palliative care, and so would not be expected to be a societal factor in the rising incidence of suicide. What was less clear is whether euthanasia of her cat made Grace herself more likely to want to die—or whether suicidal risk increases for those somehow associated with a euthanized animal.

She wrote:

> I could not grasp killing our cat for his own benefit. Likewise, nobody could understand that my killing myself was for my own benefit. They clearly thought that there was something wrong with my thinking, that it was somewhat distorted and there was something missing. But, the thing is, me killing myself was different from someone else killing me. I was not asking them to kill me. That would have been irrational. I was entirely rational. And I knew the full ramifications of what I was doing, and I was okay with that. I still am. It makes sense. If anybody really knew what I was going through and what was going on in my head, they would have wanted me to be dead, too. It was as if they thought I was missing something, but I knew that so were they.

In this new, unexpected world, a living thing can be terminated for its own benefit, or more precisely, what others perceive will be for its own benefit. Also, the living thing—once destroyed—can be replaced by a new model. Grace's sister may still cry over the cat's memory, but life goes on, and those who remember the feline can mostly be satisfied. The average third grader forgets about a cat's death, but Grace didn't. She had feared death in the abstract for as long she could remember, and now it had been actualized, not the result of a violent attack but rather of the conspiracy of her parents and their veterinarian.

Claiming that the euthanizing of Grace's cat caused the events leading to her own suicide attempts would be absurd, but the experience provided an example of how, under certain circumstances, killing a living thing might be justified. A terminally ill cat and a chronically depressed adolescent—what's the difference? Quite a lot, right? There may be less difference to some people than one might think. In 2016, a special committee of the Canadian Parliament concluded that mentally ill adolescents have a right to physician-assisted suicide, a remarkable determination given that neuroscience clearly shows that the decision-making capacity of humans does not fully develop until the middle of the third decade.[2]

If you can put a cat to sleep for a tumor, why not a human for depression? There was no doctor who would do it for Grace, and that's where the nonphysician-assisted suicide part came in. Once killing of a living thing to relieve pain becomes ethical, it soon follows that not killing to prevent suffering becomes cruel and heartless. This was a theme that Grace returned to frequently throughout the treatment.

Even though the cat could not communicate the nature and extent of its pain, its killing was justified. So it was with Grace. She could never explain her suffering, but if she could, others would understand her suicidality. She was sure of that. Psychiatric conditions including anxiety and depression create extreme distress to which its victims are unlikely to habituate. Already Grace saw suicide as an entirely rational choice—a strategy to remove the pain that had become unbearable.

An ill-advised therapist might have tried to convince Grace that her pain wasn't that bad, pointing to the wonderful things in her life and asking her to focus on these. This is in fact what I did—initially. Looking at her life from a distance, one could see much that was good. She herself could see that, at least externally, her life was a blessed one.

Her parents, happily married, loved her, and Grace got along with them, as well as with her sister. She also had many friends, and she benefitted from numerous financial and educational privileges. She enjoyed studying literature, and she knew her career path. She would become a writer and professor—if she lived, which she admitted was unlikely.

Seeing this positivity, I asked Grace how she could wish to die when there were so many reasons to live. Yet, as I emphasized the wonders surrounding her and her simultaneous inability to perceive them, her sense of failure increased, and she became more depressed.

Something was not working. Why was I pushing the happiness thing? At the time, I thought this was what you were supposed to do as a therapist, but I see now that I was reacting to my own anxiety about Grace's possible death. In doing so, I was distancing myself from an actual understanding of her pain and therefore its resolution. It was around this time that I started to read the *Tao Te Ching*, and a line from Verse 15 is applicable: "Who can gradually clarify muddy water with tranquility?"[3]

The tranquility strategy would have been to validate the pain and to note its likely impermanence. When presented with this view, she could not have denied that she might not always be in pain, even as she knew that, as long as the pain existed, she would never be able to think about anything else. As Lao Tzu says, the "men who Practiced the Way" were "Wavering, like fearing demons with clubs on all sides," and "Respectful, like being a guest."[4] The key was to be a kind of wavering, respectful guest at the edge of Grace's painful world. Such a visitor stood the best chance of gaining entrance.

She wrote:

We got a new cat. Things you love can be replaced. And, just as he was replaced, there were replacements for me. Holly could step in and be Bridget's sister.[5] And my parents would still have one daughter left. Killing myself would be okay, no matter what they said. Nobody cared about me. Why should they? They only cared about me because they were supposed to. But that wasn't enough to keep me here. Having to live with myself was worse than the people I loved having to live without me. I was in pain, and it just wasn't worth pushing through every single day. Escaping myself was the only way out.

Things you love can be replaced, which means Grace can be replaced. Here, she captured the central calculus behind "rational" suicidality: "Having to live with myself was worse than the people I loved having to live without me." She made this claim with such assurance, but implicit within the statement was a weighing of two objects, the one being found heavier. But how did she so easily dismiss the feelings of "the people I loved"? This disregard can only come with emotional disconnection, suggesting the protective effect of fostering closer relationships—that is, helping Grace understand what "the people I loved" were thinking instead of what she thought they were thinking. "They only cared about me because they were supposed to." It's a quasi-delusional statement, but one that flowed naturally from a sense of self-loathing. If Grace hated herself so intensely, why wouldn't others come to the same conclusion?

I feel like a little inside stuck in-between kind of place is pressing up against me. Oppressive. Pressive . . . ive . . . ish. Forget that. I don't know who I'm writing to, but I have some ideas. You could say that I am in between a rock and a hard place. But, you see, I am not. I'm out of hope, out of luck. I've tried one life and then another. I can try to see the light that everybody tries to show me. But it isn't there. It isn't for me. I'd say it is a mirage, but, in truth, it is more of an anti-mirage. Something everyone else can see, but not me. There for them but not for me.

Hopelessness—it stands out like a gangrenous wound. "I'm out of hope, out of luck." Having hope at all was a matter of luck to Grace, and she had rolled snake eyes in the craps game of life. To make matters worse, she saw others succeeding as they "see the light," which increased her sense of failure. She didn't think that the others were lying or trying to trick her—those would have been easier to accept. She just couldn't see the light herself—she wasn't lucky enough—and so she sank into despair. Nevertheless, the others—including me at first—continued the failing approach, worsening the problem.

Dr. Aaron Beck, the founder of cognitive behavior therapy, published a seminal paper in 1985 identifying the connection between hopelessness and suicide, noting that in a five- to ten-year follow-up of more than 200 hospitalized patients, hopelessness was present in a significant majority of the patients who eventually killed themselves.[6] It's not counterintuitive that a suicidal patient would be hopeless, but Grace's story reinforces the conclusion of Dr. Beck's study. She was hopeless and very much at risk of dying.

Some people say that death is like an eternal sleep. I sure hope not. Sleeping brings me no pleasure. I wake up more drained than I was when I went to bed the night before. I wake up restless, as if I have been running away from something. Low, as if my dreams have been nothing but pictures painted in blood, my demons. They haven't. I don't believe in demons. I don't want to believe in demons. I want to not believe in demons. If demons are true.... Death has to be the end, because, well, it's the only end in sight. Sleep is a delay tactic, but has here ventured close to an end. A cure.

Depression can be associated with increased sleep, but this was not the case with Grace. In sleep, she confronted her "demons," whatever they were. What was she running from? I still didn't know. She tried to deny them but then admitted that she wanted not to believe in them. Insomnia is correlated with suicidality in adolescents, but she didn't complain that she couldn't sleep.[7] Instead, she was tormented by something in her sleep, demons that she wished didn't exist.

Her daytime was no less difficult, as she struggled with suicidality amidst the banalities of typical adolescent life.

I can't take this SAT prep. I'm crying every session. The tears gather on the edges of my eyes and my chest tightens on the top and my throat swells weirdly so that I can only breathe the same rhythm in which I am crying, and I can't concentrate. And I can't talk, and it all comes out in a voice that is not my own. Yes, I know I have extended time, don't you? It's because I can't do this because I can't take this. And I want to run away from these people. From people. Because they can't keep me grounded because they can't reach me because I want to die. I can't get close to someone. They want me to do something because I cannot do it because I don't want to do it because I want to die because people are nice and I can't stand it because I can't take it because I don't deserve it. Can't you see me casting you off? Just leave me for myself so I can leave and have peace. And give me the peace that I won't break things for you.

The contemplative suicidalist doesn't have to appear walled off. She can be walking among the average and normal, seeming to others to be grounded, even as she stands at the ledge. They'll wonder afterward—how could she have done that? She knows there are others around her, but she is separated from them by a kind of mental haze. In the moments before the act, however, she will need to "cast" herself off progressively from those who would stop her, drifting away into oblivion. Only then can she have what she imagines will be peace.

Grace's symptoms intensified:

I'm really a wreck. I'm failing most of my classes because I barely show up to school, I can't do work at home, and I'm not in a state where I can take any assessments. The sad part is that I really don't even care anymore. I try to sleep as long as I can so that I don't have to be awake and deal with myself, but I barely can. For the first time, I don't even see myself getting better. I don't even want to at this point because there is nothing left. I don't have an appetite, and I can't sit still. My own mind and my own thoughts are hell.

I am mentoring an 11-yr-old girl from the absolute poorest part of Baltimore. She doesn't have any disability, yet she doesn't know that East Baltimore (the place she was born) is in Maryland, and that she lives in the USA. She is dead serious. It makes me feel so guilty. She has nothing, and I have so much, and I want to give it all up.

I don't feel guilty for being lucky. I feel guilty because I am trying to get out of it. Why else would I be suicidal? It feels terrible, and, in truth, I know it is. I do not deserve to be as lucky as I am. Somehow, despite all of this, I still feel lucky. I don't have a problem seeing the good things in my life. They just make no difference. The good things do not ground me in this life. They can never overcome the pain of living each and every day.

Grace's privileges intensified her shame—they should have made her feel better, but when they didn't, she felt even worse. Her suicidality then grew, followed by more shame. There was only the certainty of continual and everlasting pain.

When people become desperate enough, they try reminding me of "how well I have it." This is how guilt is forced upon me. But no amount of guilt is able to stop me from wanting to kill myself. It's as if they think that I am not aware of my own life. The guilt just makes me want to kill myself even more. It suggests that I am something wrong. I should not feel bad for wanting to kill myself. But, at the same time, I blame myself for feeling that way. I can see how much it is hurting the people who care about me.

Grace was in fact emotionally isolated, entombed already in preparation for her own death. Guilting her out of her suicidality would not work, as tempting a strategy as it might have seemed. Nevertheless, there was a role for community in her cure.

She wrote: "I can't get close to someone." She felt that she didn't deserve to get close to anyone.

But what if Grace could have been close to someone? Would she have been less likely to kill herself? It seemed possible. For Grace to die, she understood that she had to cut herself off—to perfect the "casting . . . off." She begged for it, equating it with a kind of peace. But what if the therapist didn't give her peace? What if he fought back and didn't let her off? It seemed that she might have a harder time perfecting the disconnection necessary for suicide.

Even in extremis, Grace alone couldn't separate herself. She needed to be let go and assured that she would not "break things" for the people left behind. This again raises the question of what happens when the counterparty makes very clear that the suicide *would* break things, not by making her guilty and shamed but by presenting the evidence that people care—a lot.

She continued:

Why am I taking the SAT if I am suicidal? It seems to be the question of the century. Ahh . . . sorry, moment. Because, apparently, those two things can't go together. The fact is, the SAT is part of my exit routine. I don't want the SAT score for me, I want the SAT score for everyone else. I mean my parents and my sister. I want a final thing for them to hinge on, be proud of me for, remember me as. I don't need it because I don't see myself in college. I don't see myself past the time I peel open that envelope. My sister Bridget was in the fourth or the fifth grade, before she started getting real A->F grades, she used to take my report card the moment it came in the mail, and carry it around with her everywhere. She slept with it. We almost had to pry it from her hands in the end. Her friend's brother just went to Cornell. I want Bridget to have a big sister that she can be proud of like that. And that is even more important, knowing that I won't be there. I have to end as the sister my sister can sustain on for her entire life. Even when I can't. I owe her that. It's not her fault. It's not anybody's fault. It's my fault that I can't take how much it hurts. I want to be forgotten, but I've been convinced that that's not going to happen. So I want them to remember me fondly, as someone they are proud of, because I think that will be easier for them. It has in history, hasn't it? It makes it easier on that consciousness that they are trying to groom in me.

For Grace, the SAT was to be a kind of memorial by which her parents and sister would remember her. Despite her delusional thinking on this point, she was certain that she would do well on the actual test. There was no fear of not measuring up academically, which again illustrated how suicidality might exist in situations—high academic achievement—where there appears little objective cause for discontent. The suicidal patient can measure up in some areas but not in others.

Even as she considered her SAT suicide note, she still thought about how others would perceive her. Most remarkably, she thought that the 2400 SAT score would make everything OK or at least allow her family to remember her fondly, but underlying this hypothesis was a total ignorance that her perfect SAT score would, in fact, serve to make her loss even more perplexing to her family. Absent a diary, they would not understand her pain. She wrote: "It's not my fault that I can't take how much it hurts."

What exactly was "it," and why did it hurt? Initially, I had no idea why she could be suffering so significantly. I empathized, and I tried to act as if I understood, but I felt that there had to be a reason. Dying by one's own hand requires significant effort, and simple depression didn't seem enough to cause it. There had to be the need for escape from something, although the identity of that something was unclear.

Even as her suicidality intensified, Grace retained the ability to look outside of herself, perhaps in a reflexive effort to gain perspective on her own suffering.

> It's like, sometimes, I can't stand to deal with my life, so I'd rather deal with someone else's problems. So I'll call Holly or Evie or somebody and they'll vent or whatever and I'll think how lucky they are just to have to deal with average day-to-day things like guys. Evie always calls me about some guy and ends up sobbing her heart out over the phone, and I'm like COMPOSE YOURSELF WOMAN. I mean, I guess that it might be the fact that I myself can't express my emotions to people. I always try to appear intimidating or perfect because I feel like what other people think of me is all that I have left. The most important thing in my life. It's not like I'm worried that people will think that I have problems or something. It's that, in a way, I want them to fear . . . respect me in a way. I want people to think that

I am capable of more than I am, that I have more power than I actually have.

Although Grace stated that she didn't care what others thought of her, the passage suggested the opposite. Even as she thought of the future—her death—she looked back at her past normality, when she received at least temporary validation from the approval of others. Then, she could at least be distracted from her own pain by her friends' boy troubles, or when she could play a role of one who is empowered. These are typical adolescent behaviors, and for Grace, they existed alongside imminent suicidality. The latter, however, was hidden from her friends—"I myself can't express my emotions to people"—which makes the problem of foreseeability for a clinician so challenging.

> Getting rid of the small, irritating things in life isn't going to make me less depressed. Because these are not what is making me depressed. Emptying dishwashers is not going to hurt me or make me feel more depressed because they aren't the problem. So, what is the problem? And why does the bullying make this problem worse? That has nothing to do with the problem.

At the beginning of her descent, Grace cared what others thought of her. If she were respected or feared, she would have a way to hold on. She understood that if others believed in her, she might be able to convince herself that she could believe in herself. This strategy was short-lived. For whatever reason, because of her depression or perhaps the literal or figurative accommodations that went with it at her high school, her friends turned on her as they learned of her suffering. The blood in the water, as it were, drew the sharks.

People are being stupid and judgmental. Apparently, there is reason to be jealous of me? I'm getting special treatment? Nothing is actually wrong with me? I'm lying? It is mainly Dianna, Jane, and Luanne. And then, well, I don't know. My English class and my Math class. I'm not going to list all of the names in here, but Dianna is definitely the one who gives me the most crap about it. She doesn't hate me for it, but she is jealous. Jealous? Like seriously, why would you be jealous? I have something that my classmates at Valley want. I'm smart, and they are threatened by me. Truth be told, I would give up the things that they were jealous of me for in a heartbeat. That is the entire point. I am ready to give it all up. When I kill myself, I will leave everything behind and there will be no way for me to have any regrets. That is the eternal end to my suffering. It will be worth it. No matter what I accomplish, it will never be enough to offset the pain I have to live with every single day. My only hope is that my accomplishments will serve to show that my life has produced something. It will be my final say, and I am not going to be forgotten. That in itself is not enough to keep me here but the next best thing is to be remembered for something good. It would be proof that I had maintained some control. Over and over again, people tell me that I have too much to live for, that it would be a shame for me to kill myself. They are blind to the shame that I have had to live with each and every day that I remain on this earth.

"What was the shame?" I asked her, but she would not say. She had to die because of it, but she couldn't reveal it. There was also the need for control. Had the thing chasing her from this life robbed her of that? At times, I felt like I was staring at a dying patient refusing to reveal the identity of her poison despite what had to be the ready availability of antidote.

Once Meg graduates, I am going to have so few friends at Valley it is actually ridiculous. I've looked at transferring, but it doesn't seem that is going to happen. My being like this is destroying every single relationship I have with other people. And, I mean, I can't really blame them. I am sick of people judging me, and I'm sick of everyone just hating me because I'm living through hell, and then having to deal with everything else on top of that.

The depression itself became another reason to be depressed. The depressed mind fixates on the supposed emotions of others, but Grace's perceptions were not entirely misattributions. Depression still carries stigma, causing others to back away— the exact worst thing for the suicidalist.

I am not telling anyone how bad things are because I can't get sent to the hospital and screw up my family's vacation plans. My family was always really excited to go on vacation, and they seemed to want so desperately for me share in that. I hate the "vacations" that we take as a family. For a few years, my parents kept bringing me to new destinations (most likely in the hope that they would find somewhere that would give me a little bit of a break). The last time they did that, we had gone to Spain and I had spent the bulk of the week in bed with the lights out. I was too depressed to do anything. Being in a new place did not help either. I wish that I could go on vacation without myself.

She realized that a change of scenery could do nothing to reduce her pain, but suicide could be exactly a vacation "without myself." Yet, even as she slid further into the gloom, there were moments when she doubted her path.

There was some hope that, maybe, just maybe, I had wound up living the wrong life. Then the depression must have taken hold, and swung me around at its whim. Because, perhaps, I was meant to be just one grade up. But maybe I just didn't want one year alone. Time to find a new best friend. But really every path in my life would seemingly lead back to the same place. Ireland. Land of my blood. I loved Ireland with all the hatred I had for America. When I most want to stay (in this world) forever and ever is when I see the young Irish mothers with their beautiful, wonderful Irish children. I don't want to be pregnant. But I know that would be a reason to stay. There was last year, and there was this year, and there was this hope that now is gone.

Grace was not native to the United States, and she maintained a European Union passport. This allowed her—briefly—to imagine that perhaps if she changed locations, things would be better. In her native land, she could imagine generating something or even seeing someone else generating something that would provide a reason to stay alive. Then she quickly learned that her location was irrelevant. She was indeed living the life that she was meant to have—the life of a suicidal teenager who might not make it to her twenties.

She continued:

I'm out of places to run in my head, I've been approaching the Ides, I want to die. But, where does that leave me? Right now, it leads me back to where I first wanted to die. High, high, oh my...

...to fall from the sky.

When I grow up. Well that's what I was originally going to write. Then if. But I don't want that if. I don't want that. I want it to be over, but that's not why I'm writing this.

Even as her conscious brain continued to drive her to the edge, her unconscious brain pulled her back: "When I grow up." Like a nuclear detonation sequence, many codes must be entered before the missile can be armed, let alone launched.

This is a critical point for the therapist in that one rarely will lose a patient to suicide by a single clinical mistake. In saving the patient's life, it may be enough for the therapist not to make *every* mistake.

As she sank further into hopelessness, the idea of isolation remained central to Grace's death project:

> People come and visit me. And not because my house is conveniently a 35 minute train ride to Union Station. And a pretty good place to crash. That is, in one of the five bedrooms, two of which are unused. All the hot water and free Wi-Fi in the world. Sure they are happy to see us. And the privilege of two cars to loan is just a bonus. Not that they use us, but they are family, (somewhat distant to us of course). And, as much as they love us, they aren't here for us. I need people to be here for me. It's rather an inconvenience. Convenience I mean. For them at least. What I'm trying to say isn't that people shouldn't come visit me. And I don't wish to sound unappreciative. It's more about me. And visiting people. And I know it could be a lot worse. And I know that I should just focus on being grateful for those who I do have and who I can visit. But why is it always me? And when will I see the payback? And I shouldn't want a payback. And this shouldn't be a big deal.

She looked at the people around her, and she saw them coming to her not because they wanted to see her, but because of her home's proximity to the center of Washington, D.C. She could not fathom that the visitors would come for any other reason, so far had her self-esteem fallen.

> Everybody I talk to makes it clear to me that they can see something for my life, which I am not able to see. That isn't the problem though. I can see it, and I know what I am capable of. But I don't want it. If I am offered the option to win a writing

competition or die, I will choose death. If I don't want anything, then there is nobody that can hurt me. If I can hurt myself, then nobody else can do anything that would compare.

So far, Grace's suffering had seemed primordial and somehow existing external to her relationship with anyone else. Then she introduced the idea that someone else could "hurt me." How could she end the "hurt"? By letting go and killing herself. Here, she first suggested that her suicidality might in fact mark relief from some other, as yet undefined injury. Hurting herself would provide a kind of control that heretofore had been lacking. But why was the control lacking? What had taken the control away, and why did she try to gain back the control through the act of suicide?

Until this point, I had assumed that Grace's suicidality was an act of negation designed to remove her pain, but it was now that I understood that it was also an attempt to regain control. If it were successful, she would die, but in the moments of death, she could understand that she had regained power, even if only for a second.

She continued:

They may say that I will never forgive myself. And that's exactly what I want. Not to be able to forgive myself. And then that stuff. And now I don't know where I am going. Are you suicidal? Well that's a loaded question. And definitely not the one that you should be asking. I don't want people to say that they pity me. It makes me uncomfortable because I haven't the least idea what to do. So I'm dismissive of myself.

She deserves her own page, and, really, I should write to her, really, I should. I must. It's imperative to me. I am perative to me. She is perative to me. I don't know what my life would be like without she. More like how much of it people would have left. Does she, keep me grounded? I don't know. Is the alternative so high in the sky, riding on the tips of the Monarch butterfly, that burns near the sun, and falls like ash in the snow? But it's only a season. Without the seasons. But maybe winter. Maybe I can see her in winter. Now that her parents are home. Does she know that she is the gear in the clock that runs me? Break, and I won't work. I'll antiwork. I'll anti-work. I'll start breaking down myself. From where I've broken down myself. From where I'm breaking down. By myself. By the other selves. Without a self. Breakdown without oneself. She knows what to ask, so that I can check if I'm okay. And Katastrophe has been only once, and it is over, and I will never mention it to her, ever, because I really owe her that much. I'm a flower, and I will wilt at the touch. Did I mention that she loves me? (not in a romantic way) Did she mention that I would be okay with that? She could make me okay with that?

She could make me okay with everything? (maybe even myself. myself that is, with only her.)

What was the "Katastrophe"? I had no idea. Who was "she"? As I found out later, this particular she was a friend who kept Grace alive when the treatment was not going well. Were it not for she, Grace would have never made it to my office. She would have already been dead.

This raises a point that is all too often ignored—that a simple relationship, sometimes one with another whom the patient may have met while psychiatrically hospitalized, can save the suicidalist from death much more effectively than any medical care. Nevertheless, parents of adolescents who have been hospitalized tend to prevent their children from contacting friends made on the inside—and this is often completely wrong.

Here, a friend who did little more than listen to Grace when she was upset was the single person with whom Grace was able to maintain an attachment throughout the worst of her suicidality. I never met Grace's she and never will, but the woman, a kind of psychiatric early responder, likely saved Grace's life.

But there was also a he—the he of the Katastrophe.

She wrote:

> I remember the pure wonder in the little girl's heart. And then the door opens, the light in her eyes. Glimmering. She is the harlot, charmer that she is. She knows where the trigger is, and she tells him with her eyes. Now he knows. Then. Then. The wind penetrates, and I am divided. We are bound together. The world stops. I look away, shame underneath, my eyes gone from Gaelic blue to obsidian. Am I still the child? He is in me. What they think I must not say.

Reading this passage for the first time, I was baffled, and without Grace's explanation, I would have remained so. For her, this was the central moment in her diary because it explained everything.

One day in therapy, it all came out. She was molested when she was a child, by whom she could not remember. The perpetrator was not her mother or her father, but likely a visitor, perhaps a male babysitter but maybe also a cousin. In hindsight, the offense was obvious. She had denied sexual abuse since the initial evaluation, but in my experience, victims of trauma can deny it for years before feeling comfortable enough to admit it.

"pure"—How she was before it happened.

"little girl's"—She was five or six.

"the door opens"—Her privacy is invaded.

"harlot"—She consents to being abused and is therefore responsible.

"She knows where the trigger is"—Later in the treatment,

Grace revealed that she remembered being sexually stimulated by the assault.

"I am divided"—The trauma begins.

There is much more in the passage, some sentences further suggestive of the abuse. The moment was transformative for Grace, dividing her life into two sections, before and after the mental illness. The final sentence—"What they think I must not say."—holds the most significance. "They" know about her abuse, including her complicity and consent, and as a result, Grace feels shame. She tries not to be burdened by what they think, but such thoughts will continue to vex her, driving her toward the inevitable end of death at her own hand.

She wrote:

> Want to die, be un-live?
> does death scare me?
> why do I want to leave Ireland?
> don't want to do stuff
> losing all my safeties
> anger spewing.
> There is only one way not to be depressed,
>   and that is to die.

Freud famously wrote that depression was anger turned inward, and that statement seemed especially relevant to Grace. She had been violated, and she was angry about it, then depressed. If one serially reexperienced trauma in the form of post-traumatic stress disorder, it made sense that her agitation might be so extreme that death could be seen as the only route of escape.

The initial trauma was relived continuously in mundane, unexpected occasions:

When those x-ray like machines came out a few years ago, there was a lot of unnecessary hype and hysteria—there still is. But, truth be told, I like those machines even though people can see what is underneath my clothes. Safety, of course, must come first. But, when an airport doesn't have one of those fairly new machines, they must use the old system, and the old system must mold itself to fit these new regulations. I'd much rather they see what's underneath my clothes than feel it. Of course, I was picked for further screening at the gate, way past security. My luck. In a room, closed, with a woman and a man and my sister, who was told to pretend that she was an 18-year-old witness. Feel my arms, feel my abdomen, my legs. But not my panty line. I feel uncomfortable and embarrassed, and I wanted to cry. I'm alone like the first night in the hospital.

She was searched by an airport screener in Ireland, and she flashed back to the living room of the Boston apartment where she was abused, as well as to the first psychiatric hospital where she was committed. She was triggered in part by the impropriety of a screener forcing her sister to lie about her age, just like the pedophile years earlier who broke the bond of trust and molested her.

> And then, no way to get away
> no way but to run away
> and I cry inside myself
> and I am trapped
> and to go away means to stay (in Ireland)
> They have my papers
> which for now will serve as my home
> and there is no chance
> no way out
> and one day, when the tears come
> will cry.

She considered fleeing the airport but realized that if she didn't pass security, she would need to remain in Ireland. The screener has her, as she has said earlier, between a rock and a hard place. As with her cat's death, this scene framed the future that Grace saw for herself—endless, inescapable horror. Life becomes a serial molestation, and if so, why continue to live? Suicide, like running away from the terminal, appeared the wisest solution.

With the airport incident in mind, Grace focused more clearly on what had to be done. Older males have the highest incidence of completed suicidality. When they attempt to kill themselves, they are much more likely than teenage girls to succeed. Speaking with Grace, however, I realized that she was planning with the same kind of certain efficiency.

> Time to make some decisions.
> When can I see myself.
> → senior? No
> May AP's? No
> Christmas? No
> Thanksgiving? it's getting close, but no
> First day of school? slightly
> so I'm seeing early November (2nd -> 9th)
> I'm trying to be realistic
> reservations/limits
> → October 31st: Halloween
> (limit bad associations with holidays)
> ...how? hanging (but learn how to do it right)
>   car accident (must have: me only living thing in car)
> "the original" safe method.

Her suicidality was no longer theoretical, and she left no detail unexamined. She still retained some concern for her family, e.g., when she vowed not to ruin Halloween by turning it into the anniversary of her death. She picked the first week in November. Timing, however, was just one of the many items on her pre-death checklist. She had to take care of her finances, including the cost of her burial and the disposition of her assets.

> Will: 3 bank accounts
> → Irish ones → Bridget
> American → funeral cost
> Clothing: keep or donate
> Organ donation: at least someone else
> won't lose their child.

How could someone be ready to hang herself and think about saving another child and donating clothes? It sounded implausible, but it wasn't. As she wrote earlier in the diary, "There for them but not for me." The virtues of life preservation and charity remained important for Grace—as long as she was considering the welfare of others.

As she approached what she imagined was the end, she became self-conscious. She wrote: "I don't like admitting that I have a diary any more than I like writing in one. It's what I've got to do, not what I want to do."

Why did she *have* to write? People write for many reasons, but in speaking with other writers, some of whom have been patients, I have learned that the process of writing generally provides at least some pleasure. If it didn't, why would anyone take the time to write? Did she get pleasure from the diary? Grace never answered this question. She did, however, guard her journal.

> So, when confronted by my mom about "that book that I was writing in" in Ireland, I had to lie. I had to tell her I was practicing my writing skills before AP English. But, now I'm afraid that

the next time she sees it, she won't associate it with the same level of privacy. After all, it's not just a schoolbook. It's positively, honestly terrible. I don't want her to read this, anything I'm writing, I've written. And, now, I'm getting anxious, which has only been happening these past few days. I don't want them to find the razors, and the last thing that remains is rectitude for myself. Anxiety. I've got to get rid of that.

She understood that her journal was "terrible," and if discovered would cause her to lose the "rectitude" that she had to maintain. It was a strange word for the context but suggested the danger that Grace was in. Suicide had become for her a morally correct imperative, a kind of appropriate punishment for everything preceding it. Anxiety would make her hesitate, and that she could not have.

Grace was not a grandstander or a faux suicide contemplator who wanted to be discovered, and so she had to conceal the diary. Yet, if hiding her document was so important, why write it at all? She could never explain her reasons, but I suspected that it was a means for her to gain control over her life, as was her plan for suicide.

The fall passed, and perhaps because of her anxiety, she did not kill herself. The risk, however, remained, and soon she was ready. Despite her previous statement that she would not ruin a holiday, she wrote a suicide note on New Year's Eve to her parents and sister:

Never before do I think that there has been a child who has felt so much love over the course of her life. I am not able to put into words the extreme guilt that I will always have for you. It has become increasingly difficult for me to continue to hold on. Let this be a testament to the deep regret that I feel for the indulging of my own, selfish wishes. And even though I am aware that this will in no way serve as a consolation to you, I still love you, and I always will—in life and death. I am truly sorry for all the pain that I will be the cause of. Finally, I will have peace and hope that soon you will have the same. Thank you so much for the life that you gave me.

I had never read an actual suicide note before Grace's, and I haven't read many since. I suspect few psychiatrists have read more than a handful in their careers. In the 1950s, suicidologist Edwin Shneidman discovered a file of more than 800 notes, and many of these were recently subjected to a linguistic analysis to identify any statistically significant differences between the notes of males and females. The study found that "notes from women had more indications of hopelessness, defeat-entrapment and falling short of internalized standards. In particular, the suicide notes from women more often referred to others, contained more negations, more words relevant to cognitive mechanisms and to discrepancies, and more present tense verbs."[8]

Grace's note followed the classic female pattern. It was filled with hopelessness, defeat, and a perception of a failure to measure up: "Let this be a testament to the deep regret that I feel for the indulging of my own, selfish wishes." Additionally, Grace's verbs were almost entirely in the present tense.

Somehow, she didn't die, but she remained obsessed with being dead. She wrote: "Last year, I used to draw a particular figure. It was a picture of me. Dead, and finally at peace. (It is attached.)"

There was no drawing that she ever gave me. Having failed to ask what happened to it, I suspect that she destroyed it.

Avoiding a suicide attempt, she returned to the everyday stuff of adolescence, going through the motions but also revealing why she decided not to kill herself on New Year's Eve when she was in America. She wanted to commit suicide in Ireland—a place where she had long dreamed of dying.

> I want to drown in cold ocean water. I don't want to suffer anymore. So you could argue that I would jump off of a bridge or such, but, in reality, I want to do it there. I want to do it in Ireland. I'll swim as fast as I can from the swimming bridge near my grandparents' summer home until I'm out of breath and I go down. Of course I'll do this at night so I can do it with the moon shining down. Hopefully I'll be somewhat paralyzed by the cold and I'll know that eventually my body might float into the sea.

Suicide by drowning tends to be associated with having proximity to a body of water and also with being a white male above forty years of age, which again demonstrates Grace's atypical suicidality and the clinician's necessity to avoid preconceived notions when approaching the suicidal patient.[9] An adolescent girl can kill herself by drowning, and just because she hasn't done so yet, doesn't mean that she won't. She may just be waiting for the right moment.

Grace romanticized the expected moment—"with the moon shining down"—and again seemed unaware of how her family might perceive her death. When I read this, I asked her what her grandparents would think of her killing herself near their house. She responded that they wouldn't be destroyed by it, and I explained that I thought the contrary was true. They would be devastated and never get over it, which I was certain was the case. Their own deaths might even be hastened by it. I wasn't trying to make her feel guilty but rather to present the evidence against Grace's central cognition—that no one would care whether she lived or died.

Her journal continued:

But, it is not because I want to die, it is because the reality is I don't see any point in living. The appeal that death has for me is that I won't be alive. I don't want to deal with my past, present or even live my future. I hate how I had all those problems before and now. I don't think that treatment is worth the pain when it would be so much easier to die.

There was a glimmer of hope. She realized that some kind of treatment might make her feel better. It would be painful and difficult, but it could be life-saving. Here, Grace provided an important therapeutic opportunity. No longer did she see her future as completely hopeless, even though she was suicidal. The treatment might be painful and not be worth the effort, but she was no longer certain of its futility.

After all, my future is pretty much screwed up anyways. I mean, yes, I can fix it. And, yes, I can marry and have a successful life. But I just have none of that desire any more. It isn't worth the effort. In reality, I would never overdose on pills, and my other less painful way of dying may prove slightly impossible. (drowning in the ocean). In reality, I would likely jump out of a window or slit my wrists. Maybe because then someone can save me.

When I read this, I remembered Alvarez's *The Savage God* and its detailed examination of Sylvia Plath's suicide. The author and the victim were friends, and Alvarez makes an excellent point that this popular icon of suicidality actually didn't want to die.[10] If everything had gone how the supremely intelligent Plath expected it to go, she would have been found before she died. Everything didn't go as expected.

Grace continued:

I would go from this motivation for killing myself to just wanting to die and not wanting anyone to save me. At first,

I wanted to be protected, but then I started hating myself and then I deserved to die. I started hurting myself.

The desire to be protected leads to self-loathing. This is a strange connection, but one that was omnipresent in Grace's thinking. Reaching out for help was somehow wrong and denoted weakness. This formed one of the bases of our therapy: that it was acceptable to need help from someone else and that such a need did not represent a character flaw.

At first, I was baffled by this cognition, but when the abuse became clear, her thinking made more sense. Although she couldn't determine his exact identity, she believed the perpetrator to have been a visiting relative or a caregiver—either one of them meant to protect her.

After the abuse, Grace developed the belief that wanting to be protected or even allowing someone to protect her was a tacit invitation to more abuse. The past does not necessarily repeat itself, but this is the understanding that post-traumatic stress victims lack. If Grace didn't lack it, she wouldn't still be traumatized. She would have looked at the event and realized it was a random thing that would not recur, but the post-traumatic stress disorder patient sees everything in the opposite way. The trauma is endlessly replayed, and all things associated with the initial horror generate self-loathing and fear.

So instead of outright suicide, for which she couldn't seem to muster the strength, she did the next best thing:

Cutting doesn't really hurt as much as it seems like it would. Actually, it is kind of a relief. The first time I did it I smashed a razor, and I needed a scissor to get the blades out. I ran the blade up and down my wrist, scratching it. It didn't hurt, but then again it was just a scratch. They formed raised lines on my arms and I was proud of them, possibly because now I had a reason to hurt, instead of just hurting. I remember peeking at it under my sleeve in math class. Pride. Hoping others wouldn't see. Later, I figured out that I had been using the wrong side of the blade and accidently cut myself deeply. I was afraid but relieved. I cut four more lines that day. The blood was success. It is sick, but I liked it. Finally, for the first time, I was the one who had hurt myself. I could see that I had been hurt and I knew that I was the one who did it.

Before my psychiatry training, I was unaware of how common nonsuicidal self-injury is, but it occurs with startling frequency. The latest epidemiology suggests a lifetime prevalence among preadolescents of 7.6 percent, and 14 to 24 percent among adolescents. Put another way, more than one out of every five adolescents can be expected to have caused self-injury by the age of eighteen.[11]

With cutting, Grace experienced the typical reaction—the presence of physical pain dulled her ubiquitous emotional pain. By cutting herself, she took control of the spiritual harm that she had undergone for the past decade since the abuse: "Finally, for the first time, I was the one who had hurt myself."

As she recovered, Grace frequently talked about her suicidality being an attempt to gain control. At first, this was inexplicable. How could self-inflicted death possibly be seen as a means to control? Over time, this made sense. Because the memory of the trauma grew each year, she soon saw the world as a traumatic place that could only be escaped by death. She could only maintain power if she took away the power to be hurt by everyone else. Thus, she had to kill herself, if for no other reason than the imagined deliverance.

Grace was also hurt by the people who had tried to help her, not just the perpetrator who had fondled her but also the mental health professionals who tried to help her. That I didn't hurt her as well was more chance than anything else. I was lucky enough to meet her when she was ready to tell her story, and I listened. She had little positive to say about those who preceded me:

> It's just that for the last few weeks/months, it feels like my depression (which had been getting better) is sort of starting to re-cycle to what was going on last year. And I am pretty alone with all of that because I suck at talking about my feelings. So, whenever I go to therapy, I haven't really been getting to anything useful. And, to make matters worse, my psychiatrist thinks stuff is getting better, so all he does is try to link everything back to how often I hang out with friends/guys (which isn't helpful). And now it's sort of like I am alone with all of this stuff.

> Dr. Geeringer spends a lot of time lecturing me about how I'm not depressed anymore, and how I am saying that I was suicidal just for the attention. There is no doubt in my mind that he is wrong. After all, I even have a record of all of this. He thinks that I was using the depression as a cover-up for not being able to live up to my own high expectations. As if depression is just an excuse. I can't help but wonder why he thinks that anyone would want to wish this kind of existence upon themselves. I feel like my life is over already. I don't like what I've had, and don't want what I can.

Throughout our therapy, Grace maintained anger for few of the people who had wronged her, including school bullies who had tormented her around the time that she was feeling suicidal. There were two exceptions to her lack of anger, however: her abuser and Dr. Geeringer. Although Dr. Geeringer was confronted with a difficult case, there seemed several errors to his psychotherapeutic approach, as it was presented by Grace.

First, it is unwise to suggest that a patient displays suicidality as a means to gain attention, as if such a causality mitigates the risk. If the patient wants attention and seeks to get it through suicidality, he may see a completed suicide as the way to get the most attention. Even if he doesn't really wish to die, he may succeed in suicide by accident or by attempting to spite others.

Second, attempting to convince a patient that she feels differently than how she states she feels is ill-advised. If a patient comes to a gastrointestinal doctor with complaints of stomach pain, would the physician attempt to convince him that he didn't really feel any pain at all? Here, one recognizes a bias regarding mental illness that may even be unconsciously expressed by mental health professionals—that psychiatric symptoms are somehow less real than physical ones and that just because you say you are depressed, it doesn't really mean that you are. What if Dr. Geeringer had just listened to the patient and empathized? Grace might have never come as close to death as she did.

The most galling error may have been Dr. Geeringer's suggestion that Grace's failure to meet expectations explained her depression. Although her shame at being abused drove her deep sadness, this causality did not make the depression any less real or dangerous. Perceived failure may in fact be one of the greatest drivers of suicidality, especially when one connects the incidence of suicidality with economic stress. Similarly, if a patient perceives that she has given into sexual abuse, she may feel especially like a failure.

In addition, Dr. Geeringer spoke as one who had never been depressed. If he had been, how could he have implied that Grace would fabricate such a painful syndrome for an ulterior motive?

Dr. Geeringer wants me on an antidepressant. (Which I obviously know does nothing for my depression but make me feel numb and emotionless...) . I have no idea what to do because I know that I have problems that no medication is ever going to fix. I don't want to be tricked by some medication, and never fix the underlying cause. I have to be making sense.

Grace was right. Antidepressants would never themselves erase her trauma. If they made her feel numb, the trauma would remain, but she would have lost an item to control—her sense of feeling. She might be miserable in her hyper-suicidal state, but it was *her* misery, and she could possess it.

The practice guideline for depression that has been promulgated by the American Psychiatric Association calls for the therapeutic use of antidepressants.[12] When the typical psychiatrist is treating a highly suicidal patient, he will likely follow these parameters. If he doesn't, the patient commits suicide, and the psychiatrist is sued, a jury may be more likely to return an adverse verdict against him. Most doctors would prescribe medication for severe depression; I also prescribed multiple medications to Grace, even as we began to explore her abuse.

However, she raised an interesting question that is likely relevant to at least a segment of the suicidal population. If a specific issue or trauma is driving the suicidality, the patient may realize that merely numbing himself to the problem is unlikely to provide a long-standing cure. The medication may mask the actual cause of the pathology and should, therefore, be avoided.

Then there was the issue of side effects:

I had to try some new medication to sleep on last week. That was probably one of the worst experiences of my life. It gave me intrusive suicidal thoughts, and made me even more anxious. I haven't been anxious for over a year, and I couldn't handle it. I turned extremely paranoid and seriously thought that people were following me and hiding in the corners, and closets, and behind every single door in my house. I was terrified and pretty much lived a panic attack. It got to the point where I started hearing and seeing things again. It has tapered off quite a bit, but I am still afraid of the nightmares it gave me. And to make things worse, it made me more awake than I was in the first place.

I am trying desperately to try to get Dr. Geeringer or my parents to take me off of this medication. No matter what I say, they will not listen. At first, I just told them that it was harder for me to fall asleep when I was on it. That was not enough to satisfy them, and they told me to wait a few weeks and see if that would help. Next, I opened up to them about how anxious it made me. That was still not enough. I did not want to pull the suicide card, but I had no other choice. It was what I had to do in order to stay in control of my suicidal thoughts. I did not want to become reckless. These new suicidal thoughts were intrusive, and they were not my own. I had no choice but to protect myself from being influenced by them. My well-being was my first priority. I could not let myself make any decisions if I felt that my judgment was impaired.

It is not like I am going to kill myself if I stop taking my medication. That is absolutely ridiculous. All it does is cloud my mind and restrain my function. I don't know why I get myself into situations like this. I should just have agreed to go into the hospital three weeks ago. I would have been out by now and it would all have been over.

I want to kill myself for everything I haven't done. Because I don't want to play catch up. There's nothing I want to catch up. I'm turning 16. So that's probably 1/8 of my life right there. I only get seven more. Seven more to do what? Exactly. It's just so much easier to disappear and never have to do any of this. Never, ever. Life is going to get hard, and I'm not going to have to take it. 15 years old, and I am eternity. Geeringer doesn't even see that there is something this wrong, that I am so disturbed. That I have scars on my arms.

Perhaps Grace's most damning comment about her psychiatrist is that he didn't even look at his patient's arms. Or did Dr. Geeringer unconsciously ignore the cutting, not wanting to see it?

Throughout the diary, and especially as she started to get better, Grace returned to the idea that death would be easier than life—a kind of relief where she would never have to do "any of this." What exactly was "this"? For Grace, it was continuing in a world where her trauma re-wounded her daily. Even in this deadly moment, she was still thinking rationally, however odd that may seem. She was weighing the pain of her continued existence against the imagined freedom of death.

However, what if death was not a release but rather a transformation into a much worse state? What if Grace's death meant that she would be reincarnated as an invertebrate? Or perhaps something even more unimaginable? I used this logic frequently with her, thinking that perhaps the certainty of painful life might be preferable to the uncertainty of what lay beyond. This is not exactly an original idea, as it has been shown that cancer patients facing certain death are more likely to be happy than those patients in remission.[13] Uncertainty is a principal cause of misery.

Nevertheless, even as there were glimmers of hope, she remained suicidal:

> I'm gonna cut myself some gills. Just whispers of grey across. Make them parallel. Tell me what I can see. But all I care is if you are loving me when I give myself to the sea. I'll need my gills then. Though they will burn at the touch of salt. Touch me, and I will have been touched. Touch me, and hold me when it stings. And keep on holding until my grey gills turn clean. Purged at last and peace forever at last.

I don't belong here.

I won't be long here.

I live in a world where nobody can reach me, because I don't belong where everyone else does. And that is the only way I can be safe. They cannot hurt me here.

The piscine metaphor is a strange one. Grace was often fascinated with drowning, and the idea of cutting "myself some gills" suggests the concept of becoming a dead fish, bleeding into the ocean. Alternatively, the cutting of gills could be Grace's attempt to give herself the ability to breathe, something she had lost as the depression intensified. Cutting reduces pain—and giving herself some gills might do just that.

But she doesn't necessarily die: "I'll need my gills then." She sees death less as a finality than as a transformation, in which she will somehow bleed out the grayness of her mind through the gills she has cut in her skin. She will have purged herself of the trauma.

I wish I could just get the OCD back. At least then I thought I could do something to prevent it. It was irritating, but, at the same time, a comfort. My anxiety is a way of protecting myself. And I know what I am protecting myself from.

Grace had suffered from obsessive-compulsive disorder (OCD) in the years before I met her, which I tried to integrate into my case formulation. Had the obsessions somehow made her more likely to be suicidal? The most recent meta-analysis on the connection between OCD and suicidality suggests that the former significantly increases the risk of the latter.[14] The link is not surprising; OCD is an anxiety disorder, and anxiety often leads to suicidality.

Grace, however, saw the OCD as a comfort and sort of protection. She may have thought that her trauma was driving her obsessions, and somehow these were providing a distraction, but the opposite may have been true. The OCD may have prepared her mind for the sort of obsessive thinking required for her to plan her death and seize on the idea. She wrote: "I see wounds on myself. Wounds that I haven't made."

Her abuser had made them, which returns to the idea of purging. She saw suicide as a way to cleanse herself of the foulness her life had become.

My disease will kill me. Go ahead. Bore me. To death.

For the suicidal patient, even imminent death may be another thing that is taken for granted and becomes irrelevant or tiresome.

I can't keep fighting this. I'm being completely unfair and weighing everyone else down. And, most importantly, I can't keep doing this for myself. I can't keep doing this to myself. Bridget's photography teacher commented about how I don't smile very much…haha.

Suicide becomes an act of self-care so that she doesn't keep "doing this to myself." It becomes an act of mercy, and in the same way that her cat was euthanized several years earlier, Grace will kill herself to provide relief to all involved.

15 years, and it is as if I can guide the stars. As if I am the stars. And the wanderers won't know where to go. When the light goes out, then follow her. But I can't bear all of this weight anymore. The weight of the earth, lightyears worn off. And, when you fall into despair, I'm telling you, I'm telling you, he would be there.

Her molester continually lurked in the wings, maintaining the torment, exactly when she could least defend herself.

They can't follow me. It just irritates me and makes me want to kill myself even more.

I heard music.

I almost killed myself.

Keep the fuck away.

I haven't unpacked from last time.

I don't feel like I have anyone who I can talk to and get the care I need back.

I hate when my parents try to supervise me. It freaks me out. I don't want to be around it. Too much overprotective love.

My parents' love is suffocating. They ask me to live for them, and that is what kills me. You cannot live for other people without betraying yourself. Sometimes, I think back and I remember how good it was to be able to close my door.

Despite her best attempts, Grace could not conceal her thoughts of death. This led her parents at first to seek the care of mental health professionals. Eventually, Grace's parents began to follow her, not letting her out of their sight. At times she was forbidden to close her door, or Grace's mother would sleep in her daughter's bedroom. Her parents' natural response to protect her became an increasing stressor to their daughter. They were forcing her to stay alive, and she was angry about it, as if she were being trapped and again losing control.

Sometimes, they stood over her shoulder:

I would say it started Friday with something along the lines of "I could call an ambulance, and they would take you in even without your parents' consent." Then, last night, my parents looked over my shoulder while I was on the computer writing instruction on how to find this "Final goodbye" note I wrote a few weeks ago. Ugh. I shouldn't be writing all of this down. I did not try to kill myself yesterday. I really was not planning on trying. I am under supervision, and I am sure it is because

Dr. Geeringer wants to make my life as miserable as possible in order to get me or my parents to agree to hospitalize me.

You know what? Maybe it is time for me to take a chance, a leap of faith.

Just as the suicidal patient who is hospitalized may be most likely to kill himself after his release, the close supervision of Grace may have pushed her further to the edge. Her "leap of faith," she would explain later, was to commit suicide.

Pretending to mental health professionals is okay, because then you have control. And, if you have control, maybe you can change the situation. Maybe you are really okay. I have to guard myself constantly. I cannot let anyone in.

The preceding passage is one of the most powerful in the diary. She started with the familiar concept of trying to conceal her true feelings from her caregivers, but then she realized that her ability to conceal her thoughts from Dr. Geeringer or whomever demonstrated that she had a kind of power that she had not had previously. If she had that power, however, couldn't the same power be extended to improving her life? Might it not all be black?

At almost the exact bottom, she started to look upward:

Alone, empty, that must suffice. Today, I was leaving Dr. Geeringer's office to meet Bridget, Celeste, Leigh, Mommy, and Haley. I'm not getting helped. I'm stuck in my own self-destructive thoughts. Stuck as if I am inside of myself. So I didn't see the red walk-signal, okay? It's not like it matters, not like you didn't see me coming. I came, a gentle, slow moving drone. And now I have all of these feelings of shame and embarrassment because of what it is you screamed at me.

What is your fucking problem? Do you have a fucking problem? It said don't walk.

I know that it was those first two sentences that got me. Someone suggesting I had a problem. And I did. But it wasn't my fault. I was so weak, so easy to hurt. That is vulnerability.

Well, those rules don't matter. And you don't know me, you don't know how much it breaks me, how much I want to cry. And yes, I do have issues, thank you. I hate you. I don't know what to do. & I cry.

I had so much anger, and crying was the only way I could let go. Some people scream, but I think that is for when you are mad at somebody else. Crying is for when you are mad at yourself and you just can't do it any longer. Crying is my relief. It hurts so much more when I repress it, and even more when the tears won't come. When I cry, I am less sorry for myself.

She left her psychiatrist's office ruminating about another unhelpful therapy session, and she was nearly run over in a crosswalk, having stepped out from the curb a bit too early. The driver screamed at her, and she cried, her destructive introspection interrupted. This reaction surprised me; she had talked endlessly about death, and when she had the opportunity, she didn't take it. Why not? The interaction with the irate motorist shook Grace, and she cried. She felt better, as if the contact with someone outside of her mind—even through a kind of confrontation—rescued her. She cried, and this represented a kind of release. She broke free of the repression, the grief came out, and she felt better.

This led to an important realization in the therapy. If Grace could experience some kind of emotion—even if it was extreme grief painfully articulated—she might benefit therapeutically. It goes back to the truism, cry and you'll feel better. Could it be that simple?

Grace and her parents eventually came to realize that Dr.

Geeringer's psychodynamic psychotherapy was not working, and it was recommended that she receive a treatment called dialectical behavioral therapy (DBT), which has been shown to reduce suicidality in patients with borderline personality disorder.[15] Grace did not have symptoms that suggested that condition, but the concepts of DBT—increasing distress tolerance, improving interpersonal relationships, developing emotional regulation, and mindfulness—seemed excellent strategies to help improve her condition. Still, she was skeptical.

> There are two ways to be fooled. One is to believe what isn't true. The other is to refuse to believe what is true. My main concern with DBT is that it will treat my symptoms, but not the cause. There is so much that I've talked about in therapy, but most of it has been beating around the bush. I know something that nobody else knows—well, actually, someone does know. But I don't remember who that person is. And I'm never going to get better until I tell someone about it. But I don't want it on my record—I don't want it written down. (but, ironically, I have written down just about everything.) I don't want anyone to tell my parents. I don't want to regret telling them about it—and I know I might never want to see that person again.

She understood that she had to share the abuse, and the life-saving value of the diary became apparent to her. For whatever reason, she had put everything down except the identity of her abuser. In doing so, she had broken through a significant barrier in her recovery—having recorded so much, why not capture it all? Also, she realized that the abuse was not a secret. Her abuser knew what had happened.

Along with learning she had to tell someone about her molestation, she decided that she had to leave her hometown. Always an academic achiever, despite her perceptions of failure, she applied to a highly selective university and was admitted.

Getting in has been my biggest break in years. It will be my vacation. It's not a perfect vacation; there is still so much for me to struggle with there. Still, I will not be bored there, and that will save me from my mind. It will make indefinite postponement more possible.

Her new school admission provided a distraction, and soon there were more moments of hope and the possibility of survival. She started to understand that previously horrible experiences such as high school were not entirely so.

I am going to be in the newspaper. They are writing an article about my writing. I am supposed to present on January 17th, but, if I'm in the hospital then, I will let so many people down, including the entire English department. I guess that I would just be upset with myself.

My writing gives me freedom that I have nowhere else in my life. When I am at home, I was not allowed to be in a room with the door closed. It feels so good to sit in a dark closet by myself and play with characters and plots. It gets me out of my world and distracts my mind. And, as much as I hated high school before getting into college, the English department there did give me the permission I needed to be myself. I want to enter contests for their sake, but I know that my teachers would put my needs before their own desires. Mr. Black and the other teachers want what is best for me.

Suddenly, there was a reason to work hard toward recovery, regardless of the past trauma. Grace entered a writing contest and won, and with that victory, she understood that she had the opportunity to receive significant recognition for her fiction writing. Now, she had a distraction. It is tempting to conclude that winning a literary competition was required to get Grace out of her depression, but its real value derived from its confirmation of a reality outside of her sorrow.

There was more to life than her sadness. In addition, winning the competition required her to show up, and by extension, to stay alive. She also felt an obligation to finish something she had started—specifically, entering a competition with the help of numerous mentors, and sharing her fiction with an audience. She felt she had something to communicate, something that would otherwise be lost, and this gave her another reason to live.

As she recovered, she sometimes cycled back toward mental collapse, realizing all the time that had been lost.

I should have been able to do something about this. I must have done something wrong at some point. I could have started an anti-depressant earlier, and I could have worked harder. I am on the brink of breaking down from being overly worn out and stressed. It is not the whole school stress that I have always put on myself. I can totally deal with that. But it is all this new stuff that has never been a problem before. I feel like I constantly have to look over my shoulder to make sure that nobody is going to force me into some hospital. And I absolutely dread having to see any type of mental health professional because I know that I am not going to be able to give them enough to satisfy them.

She sees "any type of mental health professional" as demanding something from her. It's a striking assessment and one that seems an exaggeration—unless one has been a patient. The mental health professional must gather information, generate a diagnosis, create a treatment plan, and prevent Grace from killing herself, even if it means using "force" to hospitalize her.

As strange as it sounds, stress is one of my favorite feelings. When I tell people that, they would laugh at me. I know that they thought I was crazy, or perhaps even that I was trying to make myself seem like I was someone bigger and stronger than I actually was. Stress clears my mind in the same way that running does. My thought processes settle into a steady rhythm, and I can drown out everything that is tugging at my mind.

Here, Grace distinguished between two types of stress: a type that she could control and a type that she couldn't. The former involved school assignments and her writing. Dr. Geeringer frequently accused Grace of grandiosity—acting "bigger and stronger than I actually was"—as when she entered the literary competition, but she felt better when she worked hard toward her goal, which she eventually achieved. The latter stress involved what she couldn't control—being molested and being involuntarily committed.

I have never had an involuntary hospitalization that has worked out well, and the reason is clear—any past disempowerment is immediately recalled when the patient is restrained and led into the hospital.

She continued:

Sometimes, people think the fact that I am doing so much schoolwork is a sign that I am, in fact, not in such a bad place. It is the opposite. I do my schoolwork so that I can escape. It allows me to get outside of myself. The more time I spend on it, the longer I can stay there. The first night in the hospital, I was terrified. I stayed awake until three in the morning translating Greek. I had no idea what else to do with myself. In the hospital, the other kids told me that I should smoke pot. I told them that I did not need to. Greek did much more for me than drugs would ever be able to do.

One can only imagine the reaction of the unit staff finding Grace laboring over a passage from Plato.

My attachment and reliance on my schoolwork was the reason the bullying hit me so deeply. The bullying happened at school, and that was the place where I had been most safe. At this point, I was unfortunately hit with a new kind of stress; one that trapped me inside of my body, and even more inside of my mind. I had nowhere I could go, and there was no way to escape it. All I could do was pour the little energy I possessed into trying to defend myself.

That Grace would be leaving her public high school for a college to which few could hope to be admitted, turned the other students even further against her. They knew she had been suicidal, and they had even laughed about it. They moved in for the kill, as it were.

It feels as if everyone is trying to get inside of my head. On the one hand, I can't help but wonder why anybody would want to do that. It is not exactly a pleasant place. As painful as it is to be in my head, it is also one of the last things that truly belongs to me. When people try to dig into my mind, it feels like an invasion, a betrayal of my need for privacy. They want to know things about me that even I didn't wish to know. I have to put my guard up so that nobody could get close enough to hurt me. There is no other way I know how to do it. I don't trust them and I have to do everything in my power to create a reason for me to be able to trust myself.

If I can't trust what I feel, then what do I have left in this world that I can rely on? The only hope I have is myself because it seems as if there is nobody else who is on my side one hundred percent of the time. People who try to argue that I don't know the truth of how I am feeling just push me further away, and give me more reason to let go. I know that I have to feel something.

Even as she planned to depart for the university, the threat of hospitalization loomed over Grace and made her worse.

I broke down on Saturday: hysterical crying, the whole deal. And then I hit the bottom. I haven't made a full day of school since, my parents are paranoid, and I can't function. Dr. Geeringer started talking about sending me back to the hospital. Just thinking about it freaks me out. I don't know how to get out of this. My thoughts just cycle over and over and over. The feeling of being trapped is what gets me. It is the push that I need to be capable of killing myself. Suicidal thoughts alone are not enough; I have to be convinced that death is the only way out.

With the last sentence of the previous entry, Grace provided another therapeutic opportunity. Give the patient just a bit of doubt that suicide is not the only option for recovery, and she may survive. There doesn't even have to be actual doubt but rather the theoretical possibility of an alternative solution. That may be enough.

I am trapped inside of my mind, but also inside of my life. Everywhere I turn, other people continue to remind me that I have no way out. I cannot even be honest about how I feel for fear that I will be threatened with the hospital or put into an outpatient program. I am trapped inside of my thoughts and now I am also trapped inside my life. If I take my own life, I will not only escape myself, but I will also finally be free of all the rest. The phrase "taking one's own life" is a better description than the term suicide itself. It is not so much about killing myself as it is about taking back my own life.

The possibility of involuntary commitment again loomed large over Grace, reminding her of her original cornering—

when she was abused. Bereft of options that might give her control, Grace looked again to suicide.

If the patient's problem stemmed from a lack of control, she would almost certainly become worse if she were forced into a psychiatric hospitalization. She would be trapped, and suicide would be one way out of that trap. Yet, despite the omnipresent threat of commitment, Grace began to have more hope, and the recovery, however interrupted, that began with her admission to college continued:

> We are moving out to Seattle for the summer so that I can take Greek at University of Washington. This does not stress me. It is one class, three lectures a week for six weeks. At night, I get to spend my summer somewhere other than Ireland and I get a whole lot more freedom to do whatever I want. That is, if I get that far.

Yet the loathing remained, as well as its consequence— self-injury.

> I cut myself after having postponed it for so long. After six months, one would think that I would know better. I cut myself as a response to turning anger inward. Doing so only intensified the self-hatred. That frustration with myself was proof that I was not trying to make myself sicker. I did not want to be depressed, and I did not truly want to hurt myself. I just had no other way to deal with being inside of my head. I did not like cutting myself. All of the arguments people gave me in order to convince me to stop cutting myself were useless. It is as though they believed that I hadn't already thought of them.

At her parents' insistence, she continued in treatment and established her first effective relationship with a therapist—a social worker whom I will call Melanie. For the first time, Grace had a collaborative exchange with a mental health professional as opposed to an adversarial one.

> Melanie used to tell me that I was beyond the point where a patient should be hospitalized. But she promised me that she would not put me in a hospital unless I came to her and told her that that was what I needed. That was so important because it meant that I did not have to keep all of these emotions inside of myself. It was a hard position for Melanie to be in, but it was the right one for her to take. If she had not given me that, then I would not have been open to her. I would have been just as suicidal as before, if not even more. The difference now was that these suicidal thoughts were not just inside of my own head. It was one less thing for me to have to be alone with.

When I met Grace and did not forcibly hospitalize her, I was triggering her favorable memories of Melanie, just as Dr. Geeringer had inadvertently stimulated memories of her abuser. Yet, even as the treatment went more favorably, the danger of reawakened trauma remained.

She wrote:

> I had this really weird phone call last night with this guy from that group therapy thing I go to. Well anyways, the guy pretty much gets me on the phone because his life sucks or whatever and wanted to talk to me about it and ends up professing his love for me. Something along the lines of, "Umm, yeah Grace. I love you. I know. Oh this is awkward. And against group rules, but I've been feeling this way for a while..." etc. etc.
>
> So that just puts me in a really shitty position, because I don't have those kinds of feelings for him, nor is he allowed to tell me that he has these feelings for me because of the rules of the group. And I know all this personal stuff about him and what he has been struggling with, and I don't want my rejection to be part of the reason if his progress slips back or whatever. But

at the same time, I can't pretend. And I just kind of want to move on and leave a lot of this behind me, like make a new life for me at college without having to field phone calls and text messages like this. And I just don't know what is the right thing to do.... I don't want to hurt anyone while trying to make things better for myself.

I talked to Melanie about it today (because there are two leaders of the group, Melanie who is my therapist and Simon, who is that guy's therapist). Anyways, she thinks we should have a sub-group session, just her and me and Simon and that guy so that I can explain myself and everyone can feel supported or something like that. But the thing is, I get home really late Saturday night. And on the following Saturday I have to leave for school early in the morning and move in that day. And in between that time, I have a bunch of bonding activities to do with Bridget (Sunday–Wednesday). And then Thursday I hang out with Haley, and Friday I just kind of want the day to myself, to finish packing and stuff. So I don't have a lot of time, and I don't want to spend the little time I have in some awkward weird therapy session over something that shouldn't have been my problem to begin with.

The crisis with the boy passed, but she was left with everything that preceded it:

I can't believe I have to live with this label on me forever. What if I have to give my medical history sometime? They ask about this kind of thing, and I would personally be inclined to lie about it. But that can't be right. And how about when I get older, and I get into a relationship with a guy and it gets serious? What is he going to think of me?

PART THREE

GRACE DID NOT DIE. We commenced weekly psychotherapy, and she revealed her abuse. Then, we started a kind of cognitive behavioral therapy called prolonged exposure (PE) therapy, and she continued her recovery. In this treatment, the patient is asked to reexperience the memory of the actual trauma, and desensitization occurs. When completed successfully, the patient still remembers the trauma but feels distanced and less affected by it. Nightmares, hypervigilance, and avoidance—the hallmarks of post-traumatic stress disorder—fade and then disappear. Grace was eventually able to discuss the abuse with little reaction. Such a transformation may seem like mere prestidigitation, but those who have been traumatized find great relief from this treatment.

Having completed prolonged exposure therapy to address the sexual molestation, she gradually recovered. The suicidality at first ebbed and then vanished. In addition to the so-called imaginal exposures of PE—that is, Grace imagining herself being abused in successively greater detail—she completed another kind of exposure by writing about her diary from the perspective of recovery. Those passages are presented here, without commentary.

BECOMING SUICIDAL is a process, and it does not happen overnight. At this point, I wanted to die, and I was just beginning to get the very first bit of initiative. I was not ready to kill myself, but I knew that I could not go on living. I was overly ready to die and I wanted to die. I just did not have the strength to do it myself. It was the intensifying self-hatred that would give me that strength.

I wish I had seen the fact that I was not failing because I was no longer capable. I was failing because I was not doing school. My parents refused to de-enroll me, so the school had to give me zeros on all assignments. I was convinced that I was no longer good for anything. All of my value was gone, and it would never come back. In fact, my not doing anything was in no way a reflection of what I could actually do. But I did not have enough hope to see that.

I was not strong enough to be there for myself, but maybe a way out would have convinced me that there was something worth sticking around for.

I have now learned that suffering does not have to be the end. There are other ways out. There have been all along. But the difference now is that I have gained the emotional capacity to pull through or even turn my life around. I know this and I can use it to face any adversity.

My life may not be okay, but I am. I can be okay regardless of whether my life is. I am here for myself. I needed people to listen to me instead of freaking out and threatening me with the hospital and outpatient programs. These are the things that trapped me. I needed for people to work with my thoughts rather than in direct opposition to them. Not acceptance, but acknowledgement. The only way I could stay here was if I truly wanted it.

Why would nobody recognize my suffering? Why couldn't they see that I was broken and that there was nobody who could heal me? I was alone. The fact that I could see myself getting out of the hospital was reason enough not to put me there in the first place. It is not to say that I wanted to kill myself any less. I just knew that it would be beyond my power to kill myself while I was in there. The hospital was just a hurdle, something I would have to get over. Putting me in there was not going to change anything. It would make other people more comfortable, but it would do nothing for me. This had to be about me, and not about putting me in a place so that other people could feel like they were doing their job. What would be the point? In being forced to postpone killing myself, I was being given more time to plan doing it right. Less emotional connection was involved in the planning when I was isolated in such a way. Passively planning suicide made me a more dangerous individual.

When I started slipping into depression, I blocked out as much emotion as possible. That way, nothing could get to me and hurt me. The only way to protect myself was to not feel. Just a year earlier, I would have been devastated when I lost my cat. The pain within myself hardened me, and the loss of this pet was nothing in comparison.

Depression is isolation from the world around you. I can't help but think about what could have been done to keep me grounded in this world. There has to be a way to pull severely depressed people into the moment so that they can experience the feelings of really being alive. So often, when you are depressed, everyone around you is just trying to make you happy. But, depression isn't just a void of happiness; it is a void of feeling in general, about anything that is going on outside of your head. The inside of your head is so deafening that you cannot hear what is going on outside of it. Yet it is quiet. You are so detached that you just cannot care anymore. When you don't feel like you are a part of this world, it is easy to progress to knowing that you don't belong here. It takes away the human connection. Human connection is the only thing that can bring you back into this world. And, when you have your trust betrayed and your innocence taken away, it is really hard to connect. After all, if you do connect with someone, they might just hurt you. The only person I had was myself, and that was also the person I hated the most.

I slipped off the edge of this world, and I was dead. The Grace that people told me was worthy of this life was gone, and they refused to see it. It was just a matter of disposing of the body that kept me trapped inside of my mind.

A lot of times, people who are trying to help get too wrapped up in their conviction that suicide is wrong. Was it wrong of me to want to kill myself? No. It wasn't. And anybody who tries to dispute that with me now has no idea what they are talking about. Anybody who tried to dispute that with me back then had no idea what they were talking about. They had lost sight of their intentions and were fighting a pointless battle. I didn't do anything wrong. It was not effective to dismiss my thoughts as irrational. It makes it seem like nobody in the world understands. Often, I found myself feeling alienated. When everyone dismisses what you say because it is "irrational," what reason do you have to stay? If your thoughts go so much against basic human nature, how close to other people are you really at all? What reason do you have to stay?

Reading this writing makes me emotional and makes me want to cry because it brings to the surface the feelings I was having at the time. My heart starts pumping and I can feel it in my arms. It skips a beat. And I feel the emotions rushing through me.

I wasn't being rational. This wasn't me. It was my illness speaking. Or...was it really? Was it me or the depression? My parents used to ask me, whenever I said something, whether it was me or my depression talking. That irritated me endlessly because I am only one person. There isn't a voice inside of my head, it is just me. Alone, inside my head. Alone. And Dr. Geeringer kept forcing upon me his theory that I was of two parts. There was a part of me who wanted to die (because I set unrealistic expectations for myself that I couldn't live up to, haha) and there was the part of me who wanted to live. He said that the part of me who wanted to live was stronger, as exemplified by the fact that I hadn't already killed myself. He was wrong, but he would not give up and admit defeat no matter what I said. I don't even think that he could admit it to himself. It was as if he was mocking me, as if he was challenging me to die. All I know is that there are not two parts of me who are struggling against each other inside of my head. I am one person, and I have one set of thoughts. I am in reality, and I realize everything that nobody thinks I can.

I knew that I could not bear going into the hospital again. I was determined to stay out of that hospital, but not determined enough to bear the thought of being alive day after day. Each day was a new agony that formed the ironically monotonous life I was being dragged through. However, at this point, I still had a certain amount of control. I had control over myself and I felt like I had control over every single aspect of killing myself. I was going to do it right. I could control the way I was going to kill myself, but not my desire to do so. That is where all of the planning was coming from. But, in the early winter of my junior year at high school, I released the last bit of that control because I just couldn't do it anymore. The images started to collect in my mind, and I could no longer hide inside of the person who I hated so much.

Many people spent a lot of time trying to understand why I wanted to kill myself. Even now, there is no question in my mind that would stand in the way of my reasoning. I was living a nightmare. There is no way to even come close to describing it. It is like being in a bubble and all of the thoughts in your mind bouncing off of the sides at crazy angles so that you hear them over and over again until your mind has run so far that you have no way of getting it back. And of your entire body feeling like it has been run over by a truck. It is almost like being dead. All of the pain, but none of the peace. Being stuck inside of the one person you despise the most.

No wonder I wanted to die. Wouldn't anyone, if they were suffering that much? The answer is supposed to be no, but I know that the real answer is yes. Anybody who felt what I felt would have wanted the same thing that I did. It was entirely rational. People were hurting me by keeping me here for their selfish reasons. They said that they were keeping me here for myself, but I knew that that was a lie. It still is. They didn't want me to live so that I would experience life; they wanted me to live so that they wouldn't experience life without me.

I had a lot of anger during this phase of my life that I was not aware of at the time. Or, at least, I placed the anger in the wrong place. I expressed unbelievable anger to my parents for moving to the United States and taking me away from Ireland.

I really felt that I was missing out on a life that I wouldn't have. I know now that it was not geographical location which was causing me to miss out on life. I didn't want to get away from the United States, I wanted to get as far away from myself as possible. However, during that stage, I liked myself a lot. (Even though I knew that I was a bad person.) So, it was hard for me to admit that it was myself I was looking to get away from. I had plans to escape, and I made these clear to my parents. I put myself in the position of power, because, I would not, under any circumstances allow anybody to reach me.

It is a little bit funny for me to now think about how much my SAT score meant to me, and how much I thought it would define me. My definition is way outside that boundary. I have become an individual, and a real person that I can be proud of. And there is value in that.

I don't know what to think about group therapy. I loved it sometimes and wanted to run away from it the rest of the time. It was nice to have a place to come where I could interact with people who also had problems—and these were people who I would never have guessed had problems in the first place. Group was fine as long as the other kids couldn't get inside of my head. Therapy is supposed to be a place where you can feel safe, but guys would get too comfortable with me and start crossing boundaries that they should never even have been near. They made me feel trapped. I was stuck in this position of wanting to protect them, but then consequentially not being able to protect myself.

Group therapy had not solved any of my problems, and I was tired of it because it seemed to just be adding even more to my plate. I was done with group therapy, just like the time I tricked my parents into giving me a break from it. This time,

I was ready to move on and have social interaction with normal people.

I never before realized how sad my thoughts really were. I can just hear in my tone, the way I placed my words, how sad I really was. And I was so emotionally numb that these feelings of sadness didn't even register with me. Looking back, I also see how awfully skewed my concept of "better" was. I was not living. I could not feel happiness. I guess that "better," for me, was a relative term. The fact that things weren't getting worse was as close as I would ever get.

I distinctly remember telling people that I wanted to die because there was nothing more I wanted out of life. There was no reason to go on. It was as if I was suggesting that I was content. Clearly, I wasn't. I think that I was afraid that things would get worse, and in that case it was better just leaving them as they were. I wanted to die in the best state possible. Once again, everything is relative.

The scars on my arms were a big symbol for me. When I first became depressed in ninth grade, my parents were extremely concerned. But, as the weeks went by, they became less and less concerned and it was apparent that they thought that I was getting better. I actually remember Dr. Geeringer having to tell them that I was not. During those weeks I became suicidal. I just thought to myself that, when my parents would question me about school and friends all that I would have to do would be to roll up my sleeve, and then they would know exactly how bad it was. It was as if the scars showed the wounds that were inside of me. The ones that only I could see.

Right now, I have way more than, so much more than I had before. I could not even have dreamt of the things that I have accomplished today. Placing first in the literary competition is beyond words, but that wasn't what I wanted. It was too far out there. I wanted to do normal teenage things. I needed things to ground me in the real world.

That is why passing my road test a week ago was such a big deal to me. It is a classic milestone, and, for me, the one that showed that I was finally catching up to the people who had left me behind. Usually, when people talk about having their hearts broken, they are referring to the experience of being rejected. My heart was broken in a vastly different way. I couldn't love anyone. I couldn't become attached. Trust was out of the question, and I could only rely on the one person I hated the most.

Just being able to be in my room by myself, with the door closed would have greatly improved my quality of life. I was alone without ever being alone. Being around other people was just humiliating.

I didn't have friends at school, and that was a huge contributing factor. There was the anxiety attack, the English teacher. All of that on top of what I already had. A broken heart, a loss of my best friend. And then the one thing I could not bring myself to talk about but eventually did.

Coming to college meant everything to me. At the same time, it was a huge gamble for my parents to take. They risked losing me even more or losing me entirely. And then there was the chance that I would get better, a chance that most people did not have enough hope to see. They had to put all of their trust in me, because that is in the end all I really have. I say "I" rather than they because there is no way to truly live for anybody else. And there is no way to live if all you do is prepare to die.

If I had not gotten better, I have no doubt in my mind that I would still want to die. And, though one never has a legal right to kill themselves, I would be turning eighteen, and there was little my parents could do to keep me from leaving and finishing the process. I had to be trusted with my own life. It was easier for me to kill myself when my life was in everybody else's hands.

Being away from my sister and my parents was really hard. At the same time, I know that it was the right thing for me. I had been around them essentially around the clock every single day for three years. I wasn't tired of them, but after going through all of that, I felt like a burden. I did not have to kill myself in order to take that weight off of their shoulders.

My parents wanted me to live for the memory they had of me, but I knew that I was no longer the same person they wanted. I would learn that that new person had the same past, and it was dealing with that past which made me okay with being the person I had been all along.

Going to college did not mean that I no longer wanted to die. It just meant that I was giving myself a chance to change my mind. I bought myself the time that I needed so that I could get to the point where I was ready to deal with and put behind me the obstacles that had hindered me for so long. I was wasting away, and I needed to put that on standby.

I could leave behind the life I was living, the person who I was, and get a completely new start. As I would soon learn, I would still have to bring myself. But I could make myself okay with that because I had control.

Control was not my problem. I was not depressed because I wanted to control everything. In fact, I had no desire to control anything at all. I did not want to live in the way that I was, but I had to try to control everything because it was the only way for me to hold on and stay in this world. I needed to survive, and that was it. Quality of life was not my primary concern. At the time, it was what I needed and I shouldn't feel bad about that. I did what I needed to do because it was all I knew how to do. I only knew how to take care of myself, and I was the only one who knew how to take care of me.

There was nobody I could talk to about any of the things that I wrote down. I did not want anybody to discount or misconstrue what was going on inside of my head. If only people had been willing to listen to me and hold what I said above their own opinions. Writing was the only way I could get it out of my head.

PART FOUR

GRACE LIVED, but for others there is no happy ending. They suffer silently, without telling family or friends, let alone psychiatrists, psychologists, advanced practice nurses, social workers, or licensed professional counselors. All too often, those with suicidality have never seen a mental health professional of any kind, as there is a lack of such clinicians as well as little national commitment to treat the growing number of suicidal people in the United States.[1] And then many kill themselves, the lessons that they might have provided on preventing suicide lost.

It is my hope that the caring professionals who have read this book have learned from my experience treating Grace, and, more importantly, from Grace's honesty and insight about her own experience. The magnitude of the suicide problem, however, is so significant that even if every professional were pursuing the exactly correct treatment, many people would still die by their own hands. For this reason, we wrote this book as much for the layperson as for the clinician.

So, if you are a layperson and you encounter a sibling, parent, colleague, neighbor, acquaintance, or lover who states he or she is suicidal—or you think is suicidal—what should you do?

1. *Never assume that a suicidal statement is being made for show.*
   Patients who are depressed but not actually at high risk for suicide may state that they wish to die, and some (like

Dr. Geeringer) may ignore these statements. Alternatively, patients may make statements of suicidality that are actually of high lethality. The trouble is that you—let alone a mental health professional—may have no idea where on that continuum a suicidalist sits. Assume she is ready to jump.

2. *Listen.* The suicidalist probably progressed to desperation because no one—or she assumed no one—would listen. If you can listen, you have a chance to break through the isolation, if only for a moment, which may be enough to prevent death. If you succeed, the person at risk may understand that she is not isolated and that there may be a reason to live. You will never convince a suicidalist in a five-minute conversation that she should not kill herself, but you may convince her to delay killing herself in that moment. What begins as a momentary delay may become an "indefinite postponement."

3. *Avoid judgment.* To those who have never felt it, the desire to kill one's self seems incomprehensible, if not ridiculous. Out of one's own fear, the listener can react with anger and even hate. These are always poor reactions, as similar reactions that the suicidalist received in his past from others may have contributed to the current suffering and hopelessness.

4. *Never think that some people are meant to die.* I have heard educated people say things like, "Well, if that had happened to me, I would probably just commit suicide." Or: "That person is so miserable he would be better off dead." We humans, however, are surprisingly bad at estimating how we would respond in future life-or-death scenarios and should therefore refrain from recommending, actively or passively, permanent choices for others based on our own assumptions. You may think that your best friend should be allowed to die if he were to become a person with quadriplegia and to become depressed, but remember that such a death wish

may be more the result of depression than quadriplegia per se. Treat the depression, and the person, despite his injury, may become no more melancholic than the average, abled person.

5. *Beware substance abuse, sexual abuse, and physical abuse.* If a suicidalist has been afflicted by any of these three conditions, she stands a dramatically higher risk of completing the suicide. The reasons for that risk could fill ten volumes, but we will only state the obvious to anyone who has suffered from these crises: they cause hopelessness, and hopelessness can cause death from suicide.

6. *Beware the suicidalist who is a military veteran or has suffered traumatic brain injury.* These characteristics may further increase the risk of completed suicide.

7. *Ask if the suicidalist has a plan and the means to kill herself.* If your neighbor tells you he wants to kill himself, it makes sense to ask whether he has a gun. If so, will he let you remove it from his house until he is feeling better and perhaps permanently? Similarly, if your daughter says that she wants to cut her wrists, it makes sense to take away the knives and razors to which she might have access. This removal might not eliminate all risk, but it may make it marginally harder to inflict self-injury—and that might be enough to save a life.

8. *Understand that suicidality is a potentially permanent response to a temporary problem.* I have treated many patients who were critically suicidal in the past but no longer are. Many of them were able to progress from suicidality to happiness. If the suicidalist can survive the present, the suicidality may resolve.

9. *Determine if the suicidalist sees a mental health professional, get the clinician's information, and make contact immediately.* The suicidalist may be angry at you, but this is likely to be temporary. Although many patients do not wish to be hos-

pitalized under any circumstances, few will be truly angry if their neighbors and friends reach out and demonstrate caring.

10. *Care.* This alone may be enough to instill hope and prevent a death. Despite all the mistakes made by me and others treating Grace, her seeing that someone *really* cared helped her to save herself.

NOTES

FOREWORD

1. ClinicalTrials.gov, https://clinicaltrials.gov.
2. "Deaths and Mortality," National Center for Health Statistics, https://www.cdc.gov/nchs/fastats/deaths.htm.
3. See, for example, Gregory K. Brown et al., "Cognitive Therapy for the Prevention of Suicide Attempts: A Randomized Controlled Trial," in the *Journal of the American Medical Association (JAMA)*, vol. 294, no. 5 (August 3, 2005): 563-70.

INTRODUCTION

1. Erin L. Fink-Miller, "Provocative Work Experiences Predict the Acquired Capability for Suicide in Physicians," *Psychiatry Research* 229 (September 30, 2015): 143-47.
2. *The Psychiatry Milestone Project*, ACGME and the American Board of Psychiatry and Neurology, July 2015, https://www.acgme.org/acgmeweb/Portals/0/PDFs/Milestones/PsychiatryMilestones.pdf.
3. "Suicide Statistics" (November 2015), American Foundation for Suicide Prevention, http://www.afsp.org/understanding-suicide/facts-and-figures; Arialdi M. Miniño et al., "Deaths: Final Data for 2000," *National Vital Statistics Reports*, vol. 50, no. 15 (September 16, 2002), https://www.cdc.gov/nchs/data/nvsr/nvsr50/nvsr50_15.pdf; Sally C. Curtin, Margaret Warner, and Holly Hedegaard, "Increase in Suicide in the United States, 1999-2014," NCHS Data Brief no. 241 (April 2016): 1-8, https://www.cdc.gov/nchs/products/databriefs/db241.htm.
4. "Deaths: Final Data for 2013," *National Vital Statistics Reports*, vol. 62, no. 2 (February 16, 2016), http://www.cdc.gov/nchs/data/nvsr/nvsr64/nvsr64_02.pdf.
5. E. W. Fleegler et al., "Firearm Legislation and Firearm-Related Fatalities in the United States," *JAMA Internal Medicine*, vol. 173, no. 9 (May 13, 2013): 732-40.
6. Lacking a word to denote someone who either contemplates or completes a suicide, I use the word *suicidalist*.
7. Anne Case and Angus Deaton, "Rising Morbidity and Mortality in Midlife among White Non-Hispanic Americans in the 21st Century," *Proceedings of*

the *National Academy of Sciences of the United States of America*, vol. 112, no. 49 (December 8, 2015): 15078–83.

8. "Employment Projections," Bureau of Labor Statistics, last modified April 20, 2017, http://www.bls.gov/emp/ep_chart_001.htm.

9. Allison Milner, Andrew Page, and Anthony D. LaMontagne, "Long-Term Unemployment and Suicide: A Systematic Review and Meta-Analysis," *PLOS ONE*, vol. 8, no. 1 (January 16, 2013): e51333.

10. Suzanne Petroni, Vikram Patel, and George Patton, "Why Is Suicide the Leading Killer of Older Adolescent Girls?," *The Lancet*, vol. 386, no. 10008 (November 21, 2015): 2031–32.

11. H. Sampasa-Kanyinga and H. A. Hamilton, "Social Networking Sites and Mental Health Problems in Adolescents: The Mediating Role of Cyberbullying Victimization," *European Psychiatry*, vol. 30, no. 8 (November 2015): 1021–27.

12. A. Preti, "Animal Model and Neurobiology of Suicide," *Progress in Neuro-Psychopharmacology & Biological Psychiatry*, vol. 35, no. 4 (June 1, 2011): 818–30.

13. N. Oexle et al., "Mental Illness Stigma, Secrecy and Suicidal Ideation," *Epidemiology and Psychiatric Sciences*, vol. 26, no. 1 (February 2017): 53–60.

PART ONE

1. G. B. Parker and R. K. Graham, "Determinants of Treatment-Resistant Depression: The Salience of Benzodiazepines," *The Journal of Nervous & Mental Disease*, vol. 203, no. 9 (September 2015): 659–63.

2. Samuel Shem, *The House of God* (New York: Berkley, 2010), 361. Certain aphorisms from Shem's novel describing one doctor's journey through internship have become clinical pearls—bits of medical lore that, even though unproven, offer guidance to a physician beset with uncertainty.

3. Daniel Pagnin et al., "Efficacy of ECT in Depression: A Meta-Analytic Review," *The Journal of ECT*, vol. 20, no. 1 (March 2004): 13–20.

4. Sylvia Plath, *The Unabridged Journals of Sylvia Plath*, ed. Karen V. Kukil (New York: Anchor, 2000), 668.

5. David Lester, "Understanding Suicide through Studies of Diaries: The Case of Cesare Pavese," *Archives of Suicide Research*, vol. 10, no. 3 (2006): 295–302.

PART TWO

1. Jitender Sareen et al., "Anxiety Disorders and Risk for Suicidal Ideation and Suicide Attempts: A Population-Based Longitudinal Study of Adults," *Archives of General Psychiatry*, vol. 62, no. 11 (2005): 1249–57.

2. Kathleen Harris, "Mature Minors, Mentally Ill Should Have Right to Doctor-Assisted Death, Report Advises," *CBC News*, last modified April 21, 2016, www.cbc.ca/news/politics/assisted-dying-committee-recommendations-1.3463392.

3. Lao Tzu, *Tao Te Ching*, trans. William Scott Wilson (Boston, MA: Shambhala Publications, 2010), 25.

4. Ibid.

5. Bridget (not her real name) is Grace's sister.

6. A. T. Beck et al., "Hopelessness and Eventual Suicide: A 10-year Prospective Study of Patients Hospitalized with Suicidal Ideation," *The American Journal of Psychiatry*, vol. 142, no. 5 (May 1985): 559–63.

7. Maria Zschoche and Angelika Anita Schlarb, "Is There an Association between Insomnia Symptoms, Aggressive Behavior, and Suicidality in Adolescents?," *Adolescent Health, Medicine and Therapeutics*, vol. 6 (2015): 29–36.

8. D. Lester and A. Leenaars, "A Comparison of Suicide Notes Written by Men and Women," *Death Studies*, vol. 40, no. 3 (2016): 201–3.

9. D. P. Wirthwein, J. J. Barnard, and J. A. Prahlow, "Suicide by Drowning: A 20-Year Review," *Journal of Forensic Sciences*, vol. 47, no. 1 (January 2002): 131–36.

10. A. Alvarez, *The Savage God: A Study of Suicide* (New York: W. W. Norton & Company, 1971), 49.

11. S. P. Lewis and N. L. Heath, "Nonsuicidal Self-Injury among Youth," *The Journal of Pediatrics*, vol. 166, no. 3 (March 2015): 526–30.

12. "Practice Guideline for the Treatment of Patients with Major Depressive Disorder," third edition (November 2010), PsychiatryOnline, http://psychiatry online.org/pb/assets/raw/sitewide/practice_guidelines/guidelines/mdd.pdf.

13. Paul Dolan, *Happiness by Design* (New York: Hudson Street Press, 2014), 66.

14. I. Angelakis et al., "Suicidality in Obsessive Compulsive Disorder (OCD): A Systematic Review and Meta-analysis," *Clinical Psychology Review* 39 (July 2015): 1–15.

15. M. M. Linehan et al., "Dialectical Behavior Therapy for High Suicide Risk in Individuals with Borderline Personality Disorder: A Randomized Clinical Trial and Component Analysis," *JAMA Psychiatry*, vol. 72, no. 5 (May 2015): 475–82.

PART FOUR

1. Thomas P. Weil, "Insufficient Dollars and Qualified Personnel to Meet United States Mental Health Needs," *The Journal of Nervous and Mental Disease*, vol. 203, no. 4 (April 2015): 233–40.